Thinking

Think Better and Change Your Life

By Charles D. Patton

THINKING: THINK BETTER AND CHANGE YOUR LIFE

ISBN: 978-1-963809-56-5 (Paperback: Ingram Spark)
Published by: Short Mystery Press
Orlando, Florida, USA
First Edition

This is a work of nonfiction. While every effort has been made to ensure accuracy, some names and identifying details may have been changed to protect privacy. The author and publisher disclaim liability for any loss or damage caused by the use or misuse of information contained in this book.

Cover Design: Book Design Company
Editing: Author / ChatGPT
Printed in the United States
10 9 8 7 6 5 4 3 2 1

Contents

Preface

Our thoughts shape us, so think deliberately to become who you wish to be.

The human brain has an extraordinary ability: it can observe its own thoughts. Yet most people rarely use this gift. They drift through life reacting to events, letting outside influences and emotions guide their decisions. Thinking, for many, is something that just happens. But for those who want more from life, who wish to direct their minds instead of being directed by them, thinking can become a discipline as real and powerful as any craft or profession.

Who is responsible for the quality of your thoughts? The answer is simple: you are. Tony Robbins once said, "You've got to realize that you must take conscious control of running your own mind; otherwise, you're going to be at the mercy of whatever is happening around you." Thinking is not a talent reserved for a few; it is a practice available to anyone willing to cultivate it. Coaches, teachers, and books can guide you, but mastery of thought must be earned through awareness and consistent effort.

Consider a few examples: a master mechanic diagnosing an engine by sound, a surgeon teaching calm precision in an operating room, a diver reading subtle currents, or a woodworker shaping perfect joints by instinct. None may be called "geniuses" in the traditional sense, yet each has developed a level of awareness that extends beyond technique. They have learned to think deeply, to see patterns, anticipate outcomes, and trust judgment refined through experience. That is the kind of thinking this book will help you build.

Learning from others, however, carries a risk: the temptation to let experts do your thinking for you. Advice and instruction are valuable only when balanced with personal reasoning. True understanding begins when you stop accepting

2

ideas without question and start testing them against your own observation. The goal is not to reject guidance but to refine it, to think *with* others, not *through* them.

One of the great teachers of this art was the French priest and writer Ernest Dimnet, often called "the father of the art of thinking." His 1928 book *The Art of Thinking* influenced generations and remains relevant today. Dimnet warned that too many people borrow their ideas from leaders, reformers, and public voices, allowing those voices to replace their own. His message was clear: if you do not think for yourself, you surrender your individuality.

In authoring this book, I have drawn inspiration from Dimnet's vision and adapted many of his principles for a modern world where information is constant, and distraction endless. He believed that every generation must rediscover thinking for itself, that timeless truths must be reexamined, not repeated. Following that spirit, I have expanded, simplified, and challenged his foundation where needed, while keeping his central purpose intact.

Ultimately, this book cannot think for you. It can only serve as a guide, a framework for observing how your thoughts form, how they shape your behavior, and how they can be restructured to serve your goals. Your progress will depend on your honesty and discipline. Approach these pages with curiosity and courage, and you may find that your mind is far more capable than you have ever imagined.

Introduction

Most people let their thoughts wander wherever life takes them, but those who learn to direct their thinking discover a power that changes everything. If you seek to take control of your thoughts and, in doing so, achieve more than you imagined, the ideas in this book can be transformative.

This is not a book of inspiration or hidden secrets. Its purpose is practical: to help you stop depending on external voices and start listening to your own. You are the central figure in this work, and your task is to gain control over your thoughts and set a deliberate course for your life.

Consider this: how often do you think about the process of thinking itself? Are you aware of your thoughts, or do you simply react to what you see and hear? When discussing politics, ethics, or social issues, do you repeat what others have said, or do you build your own conclusions? Can you defend your views with facts you have examined and verified? The chapters ahead will help you strengthen your independence of thought and your confidence in reasoning for yourself.

Learning to manage your thoughts brings lasting benefits such as greater happiness, self-confidence, clarity, and purpose. The results depend entirely on how well you apply the ideas presented here. Thinking, when done with intention, can transform you into a more complete version of yourself. The sooner you begin and commit to the process, the greater the impact will be.

Many find deep thinking difficult or even uncomfortable, preferring the ease of surface thoughts. Yet thinking is an ongoing process for everyone. The question is not whether you think, but how, and whether you guide your thoughts or allow them to be guided by external forces. Directed or controlled thinking, as described in this book, is a discipline that has helped ordinary people reach extraordinary goals.

Without direction, thoughts drift aimlessly, and for many that seems enough. Even those who occasionally take control may do so inconsistently. Some, such as yoga or meditation practitioners, seek clarity through stillness by quieting thought to see the mind more clearly. Yet even this is a form of thinking: an intentional act of awareness.

Thinking defines who you are. Thinking is being. We are inseparable from our thoughts, and being oneself depends entirely on what one thinks. If you aren't thinking, you aren't truly alive. Even those who have awakened from comas describe vivid moments of awareness and observation. Our thoughts are uniquely our own; they shape our identity, our emotions, and our experience of life.

If you are what you eat, then even more profoundly, you are what you think. Our thoughts don't just describe us, they create us.

In our time, the challenge of thinking has grown more complex. Information arrives faster than we can evaluate it. News, entertainment, and opinions compete for our attention, and social media rewards reaction more than reflection. Artificial intelligence now mirrors our words and patterns, offering answers before we have time to ask the right questions. In this environment, independent thought is not automatic; it must be chosen. The ability to pause, question, and decide for oneself has become a modern form of courage. This book is an invitation to reclaim that courage and to rediscover the power of your own mind.

Chapter 1: What Are Thoughts?

Flowing Images

Thoughts are the flowing images of the mind, a continuous film silently running behind every moment of consciousness. They move as scenes do on a screen, each one connecting to the next, creating meaning through sequence and emotion. This flow, called a Flux, forms the living current of awareness that never stops moving. Within it exist images, fragments of sound, echoes of feelings, and faint traces of memory, each blending into the next in ways no scientist has yet fully mapped.

Sometimes your thoughts are clear and detailed, as if projected in high definition. At other times, they are dim and fleeting, like smoke that cannot be grasped. The mind links image to image through association. You might think of a friend, which reminds you of a conversation, which leads to an idea that changes your mood. This unseen choreography is how consciousness weaves the fabric of your identity.

Science can describe what parts of the brain are active, but not what the mind actually *is*. We know that we can imagine sounds and smells, yet we do not literally hear or smell within thought. A melody might replay endlessly in your mind, but the sound is a ghost, your brain reproducing remembered sensation. A certain fragrance can carry you back decades, stirring images, voices, and feelings as vivid as if no time had passed. Thoughts, then, are the blending of perception, imagination, and memory into a stream that defines how we experience life.

Every person's Flux is unique. A painter may think in colors, a musician in tones, an athlete in physical sensations, a philosopher in language. Yet the process is the same: a constant exchange between perception and memory. Imagination creates what has not yet been seen, while memory re-creates what once was. Between these two forces lies all creative thought.

In rare moments, this natural current narrows into a focused channel known as Flow. Flow is total concentration, where all of your attention gathers around one activity and time itself seems to dissolve. You may have felt this while writing, performing, or even fixing something with complete absorption. The psychologist Mihály Csíkszentmihályi described it as full involvement and joy in the process itself.

Artists, surgeons, climbers, and craftsmen all know this state. Everything feels effortless because thought and action have become one. Flow is not limited to achievement, it is available to anyone who gives full attention to the present task. Ancient traditions recognized it as well. In Zen practice, a tea ceremony, archery, or even sweeping the floor can become Flow when performed with complete presence. At its highest level, Flow and meditation meet, producing the peace known as Nirvana.

Flow borders closely on another mental state: Hyperfocus. Where Flow brings balance and fulfillment, Hyperfocus can narrow attention so sharply that perspective disappears. It may appear as obsession, as when someone becomes lost in a detail or a repetitive task. Hyperfocus can be productive for a time, but when it excludes awareness of life's wider balance, it becomes a trap. Addiction lies one step further, where brain chemistry enslaves attention and desire.

Flux, Flow, Hyperfocus, and Addiction form a spectrum of mental intensity, ranging from free, balanced thought to fixation that consumes the self. The art of thinking is learning to stay in the healthy middle of that spectrum; focused yet open, aware yet flexible.

Thoughts are the invisible current of your being. They capture every experience, control your actions, and collectively shape who you are becoming. The quality of those thoughts determines the quality of your life. If you fill your mind with confusion, resentment, or fear, those images will find expression in your speech and behavior. But if you fill it with clarity, purpose, and truth, those same qualities will become visible in all you do.

Thoughts Never Stop

Thinking is constant. Whether you are awake or asleep, thoughts continue their movement, shifting from image to image without rest. Even when you try to silence them, they reappear, sooner or later, the current resumes its flow. Only with training can you hold your mind still for more than a few seconds.

These thoughts can be vivid or abstract, real or imaginary, comforting or troubling. They move at different speeds, sometimes in layers. You might be driving and planning dinner, listening to a song while remembering a friend, or reading while half-dreaming about tomorrow's tasks. Though it seems simultaneous, the brain is actually switching focus rapidly between threads. True multitasking is an illusion.

The mind continues to think even in sleep. Dreams, hallucinations, and moments of sudden insight show that mental processing never stops. During REM sleep, the brain reorganizes experiences, forming connections we might not make while awake. That is why you can awaken with a solution to a problem that puzzled you the day before. Sleep, far from being an interruption of thought, is a different kind of thinking, one that reveals how deeply your mind works beyond your control.

Daydreaming is another form of silent problem-solving. The wandering mind connects ideas that structured reasoning often overlooks. Many inventions and artistic works have emerged from such idle mental drift. The mind at play often discovers what the mind at work cannot. Albert Einstein once said that imagination is more important than knowledge, because knowledge defines what we already know, but imagination opens the door to what we do not.

Thoughts also form emotional clusters called complexes. A smell might recall your grandmother's kitchen; a song might return you to a lost love. These clusters hold feelings that can shape how you interpret new experiences. Understanding these patterns helps you manage emotion and perception, for each memory carries its own tone and influence.

Sleep, meanwhile, has a cleansing function. After rest, the mind seems refreshed, old problems lose weight, and clarity returns. Neuroscientists believe the brain physically washes itself during deep sleep, removing waste chemicals and reorganizing memory. The result is mental order, a fresh start each morning.

Thoughts can be logical or illogical, linear or chaotic. Logic can be taught, but thinking itself is natural and universal. Under stress, illness, or chemical influence, the orderly flow can fragment into confusion, producing distorted images or hallucinations. Yet even in such disarray, the mind is doing what it does best, trying to make sense of the world.

Each train of thought begins with a spark: a sensation, an image, a phrase, or an emotion. The smell of pine may recall a forest walk; a single word may lead to a memory that spirals into reflection. Thoughts can move backward into the past or forward into the imagined future. They may leap quickly or crawl slowly, and you might be aware of only fragments. Yet even the hidden parts of thought shape your feelings and choices.

Some sequences of thought end in decision, others simply fade. Occasionally, they bring discovery. Isaac Newton's insight into gravity came, in his words, by "thinking about it all the time." In truth, thought never ends, it simply changes direction.

Images eventually evolve into abstract ideas. The mind seeks to translate them into language so they can be shared, but this translation is imperfect. Words simplify what the mind perceives, and no two people interpret them exactly the same way. Misunderstanding, therefore, is not only common but inevitable. To think clearly is to bridge that gap, to express the inner image so precisely that others can see it too.

Mental Patterns

Each thought leaves a trace. When repeated, these traces form mental patterns, pathways in the brain that strengthen with use. This is how habits, skills, and beliefs are created. The more often you repeat an action or idea, the more easily it arises again.

These patterns serve you when they simplify life: walking, reading, driving, or tying your shoes. Yet they also trap you when they form limiting beliefs. Someone who has failed repeatedly may build a pattern of doubt that replays every time they attempt something new. To break such a pattern, you must deliberately create a new one through conscious experience and repetition.

Neuroscientists call this process neuroplasticity, the brain's ability to rewire itself through learning. Every time you practice a new thought or behavior, you carve a new path in the mind. The more you travel that path, the stronger it becomes, until it replaces the old one. Change, therefore, is not only possible, it is biological.

Learning to recognize your mental patterns is the first step toward mastering them. Ask yourself: do your thoughts serve your goals, or do they keep you where you are? The brain's efficiency is both its strength and its danger. What it repeats becomes automatic, for better or worse. The art of thinking well is learning which thoughts deserve repetition.

Our Brains Cannot Focus on Two Sensory Inputs Simultaneously

Research shows that when you focus on one sensory input, hearing a sound, feeling a texture, or looking at an image, your brain waves stay steady and thought continues smoothly. But when you try to divide your attention between two different inputs, the brain falters. Attention flickers and thought momentarily pauses.

Pickpockets have exploited this for centuries. One person bumps into you and apologizes, drawing your eyes and words, while another lifts your wallet. In that instant, your attention is elsewhere. The lesson is simple: divided focus weakens awareness. Concentration is power.

Can You Reflect and Act at the Same Time?

Not quite. Reflection and action are like inhaling and exhaling, you cannot do both at once, but both are necessary. Thought guides action, and action refines thought. Skilled people move between them rapidly, appearing to do both, but in truth they alternate focus at lightning speed. Mastering this rhythm is one of the hallmarks of effective thinking.

Left Brain and Right Brain

The brain's two hemispheres work as partners. The left side is analytical, breaking information into parts, while the right is intuitive, seeing the whole. Logic lives on one side, imagination on the other.

Vadim Kotelnikov's research helps explain why some people excel at invention but stumble at execution, or why others organize efficiently but rarely create something new. The key lies not in choosing sides but in integration. Einstein, for example, used mathematical logic to express ideas born from visual imagination. Leonardo da Vinci blended engineering with art. The most powerful minds are those that allow both hemispheres to cooperate, reason feeding creativity, and creativity renewing reason.

Limited Attention Span

Robert Frost once quipped that "the brain is a wonderful organ. It starts working the moment you get up in the morning and does not stop until you get into the office." Humor aside, attention is limited. The mind can only hold a few ideas in focus at once, and that narrow beam of awareness is both a gift and a restriction. It keeps your thoughts coherent but also confines them to familiar ground.

Dr. Edward DeBono emphasized that our minds rely on established patterns because they are efficient. Each time you solve a problem a certain way, your brain strengthens that route, making it easier to reuse. Over time, you begin to think along the same lines automatically. This is why people often repeat the same mistakes, they are traveling well-worn mental roads.

DeBono's idea of lateral thinking challenges this habit. To think laterally means stepping off the usual path, approaching a question from a new direction. It is how creative breakthroughs happen. For instance, Alexander Fleming discovered penicillin because he noticed mold killing bacteria on a neglected petri dish, something most would have thrown away. Lateral thinking begins where ordinary thinking stops.

To practice it, try this: take a familiar problem and deliberately describe it backward, upside down, or from another person's point of view. Or combine unrelated ideas, a technique called forced association, to see what patterns emerge. By doing so, you stretch the boundaries of what your mind expects and invite innovation to appear.

Multiply Your Inventive Thinking Power

When faced with a challenge, do not wait until pressure builds. Engage your subconscious mind early. Start by gathering facts, asking questions, and sketching out ideas. Then let the problem rest. Your subconscious will continue to process it quietly, linking elements you may not consciously notice.

Many of history's discoveries were born this way. Mendeleev dreamed of the periodic table. Paul McCartney heard the melody of "Yesterday" in his sleep. The conscious mind works slowly, but the subconscious is lightning fast. Feed it clear information, what you want to solve and why it matters, and it will deliver the how when the time is right.

As Vadim Kotelnikov wrote, "The more you practice this, the better and faster ideas you will receive from your subconscious mind." The best thinkers learn to trust this partnership, alternating deliberate focus with relaxed openness.

Memory and Its Capacity

People learn in two main ways. Some learn cerebrally, through reading, study, and analysis. Others learn physically, through experience and motion. A physicist solving equations and a dancer mastering a performance both engage memory, but in different forms.

Short-term memory holds only a few items for seconds before they fade. Long-term memory stores information through repetition or emotion. Emotion marks memory deeply, which is why we remember events tied to joy, shock, or sorrow. To strengthen short-term memory, repeat information aloud, group related ideas, or use visualization. Imagine placing each idea into a mental space, a room, a shelf, or a doorway, and recall it by walking through that space in your mind.

Working memory is the space where thinking happens. It allows you to juggle information, compare ideas, and connect them in new ways. The larger and more flexible your working memory, the greater your creative capacity. In physical learning, repetition builds muscle memory so that the body acts without conscious command. Talent may spark interest, but persistence completes mastery.

Memory and creativity are partners. Knowledge gives material to work with; imagination rearranges it into something new. Artists, scientists, and leaders all rely on this balance. The sculptor remembers the feel of stone, the mathematician recalls equations, and the leader remembers lessons from experience, all transforming memory into creation.

Persistence, above all, determines how far these powers reach. Every thinker faces resistance, distraction, and doubt. Persistence keeps attention steady long enough for insight to emerge. Talent begins the journey, but endurance finishes it.

Thought and memory together form the foundation of who you are. They hold the record of your past and the blueprint of your future. To think well is to use both consciously, to notice what your mind is doing, to shape it deliberately, and to direct it toward what matters most. Thinking is not simply what the brain does. It is the art of guiding your mind toward truth, purpose, and possibility.

Chapter 2: The Nature and Kinds of Thinking

Different kinds of thoughts can be given different labels. Francis Lucile, a spiritual teacher, identified three broad types:

1. **Practical Thoughts** – thoughts about our day-to-day activities.
2. **Personal Identity Thoughts** – thoughts about who we are.
3. **Thoughts about the Ultimate** – thoughts about God, the Universe, or the meaning of existence.

These categories are not isolated boxes but fluid states of mind. In a single hour, a person might move through all three: planning dinner, questioning a career choice, and then marveling at the night sky. The movement between them shows how dynamic the mind truly is.

Thoughts can generally be categorized as good or bad, though a wide gray area often blurs that line. Understanding the difference requires navigating subtle shades of motive, context, and consequence. A thought can align with good or evil; in some cases, it defines the very concepts of good and evil themselves.

Some thoughts involve things within our control, choices we can act upon today. Others concern matters we can't yet influence because of timing, authority, or circumstance. This distinction is crucial: many people exhaust themselves worrying about what they cannot yet change. Recognizing the difference between controllable and uncontrollable thoughts is a cornerstone of mental peace.

Most thoughts are self-centered. They revolve around insecurity, criticism, and frustration, or desires such as approval, pleasure, or possession. These thoughts often appear in disguise: ambition masquerading as purpose, fear posing as caution, envy cloaked in admiration. Yet the same mind is capable of selfless thought, concern for another's safety, compassion for a stranger, a wish to improve the common good. The mind, like a lens, can focus either inward or outward depending on where you point it.

Ideas: The Product of Thought

It's essential to recognize that while we often treat *thoughts* and *ideas* as synonymous, an idea is a refined form of thought. A single spark of awareness becomes an idea when it takes shape, gains direction, and carries potential for action.

Ideas arise when memory, observation, and imagination converge. A craftsman imagines a better tool, a teacher sees a clearer way to explain, a scientist connects two unrelated facts and glimpses a law of nature. That fusion of logic and imagination transforms raw thought into invention.

Sometimes ideas surface suddenly, flashes of insight that seem to appear from nowhere. At other times, they emerge from long concentration. Isaac Newton's "apple" story, whether legend or not, symbolizes how the mind's quiet attention can meet a moment of chance and produce discovery.

An idea's fate depends on what happens next. Some fade quickly; others evolve into lifelong pursuits. Passion keeps an idea alive through obstacles, while obsession turns it into a master that enslaves its creator. The dividing line between passion and obsession is control: passion serves your purpose; obsession consumes it.

Our senses often spark thoughts, the smell of bread can trigger childhood memories; the sight of a sunset can inspire poetry; the sound of thunder may prompt reflection on our place in nature. But thoughts also emerge from the deeper mind. They can be born from dreams, unconscious pattern-recognition, or emotional currents we barely perceive. Desperation, joy, or fear may surface as new ideas.

Every idea eventually seeks resolution. It can be acted upon, analyzed, postponed, or dismissed. Even unethical impulses, like envy or revenge, are subject to the same rule: they either fade through inaction or grow through attention. Awareness itself is a moral filter. To notice a destructive idea and let it pass is an act of discipline as great as performing a noble deed.

Reflection

Reflection is the workshop of the mind, the place where raw thought is refined into understanding. Madame Maintenon described it as "thinking attentively of the same thing several times over." It is not circular worrying; it is deliberate reconsideration from multiple angles.

Imagine a sculptor walking around a block of marble, viewing it from every side before carving. Reflection is that mental circling, testing how a thought looks in light, shadow, and distance.

We often associate reflection with mirrors, and the analogy is apt. Just as a mirror reveals your outward appearance, mental reflection reveals your inner form, your motives, fears, and hopes. It turns experience into feedback. Without that feedback, we repeat mistakes endlessly, expecting different results.

Reflection differs from rumination. Rumination is the mind replaying an event in search of comfort or blame. Reflection, by contrast, is purposeful review aimed at truth. It asks, *What did I learn? How can I apply it?* It transforms emotion into insight.

Philosophers from Confucius to Marcus Aurelius treated reflection as a daily duty. Confucius advised reviewing one's actions each evening to see whether virtue had guided the day. Marcus wrote his reflections as meditations that later guided generations. Reflection connects experience to conscience.

In modern life, reflection is too often replaced by distraction. Our devices fill every spare moment, leaving no silence in which thought can return to itself. Yet it is precisely in those quiet intervals, while driving without music, walking without a phone, or sitting before sleep, that the mind digests what it has taken in. Reflection is mental metabolism; without it, ideas accumulate but never nourish.

Practically, reflection can be cultivated through journaling, quiet walks, or deliberate pauses after major events. Ask simple questions: *What surprised me? What would I change? What pattern do I see forming?* Such questions turn memory into guidance.

Ultimately, reflection teaches humility. It reminds us that knowledge is temporary, and understanding is earned through continual reconsideration.

Kinds of Thinking

A thought is the product of thinking, the intentional use of the mind to reach or reveal something. Thinking gives shape to imagination, weight to memory, and direction to feeling.

Thinking is both art and discipline. It can be trained like a muscle or left to wander like an untamed animal. The difference between a sharp thinker and a dull one is practice, not birthright. Every mind improves through use.

There are many varieties of thinking: scientific, mathematical, historical, anthropological, economic, moral, and philosophical. Each represents a particular lens through which the mind examines reality.

- **Scientific thinking** tests ideas through observation and experiment.
- **Mathematical thinking** seeks pattern and precision.
- **Historical thinking** draws wisdom from the record of human experience.
- **Moral thinking** weighs right and wrong in the light of conscience.
- **Philosophical thinking** questions the assumptions beneath all others.

In daily life, we blend these forms without naming them. When a parent plans a household budget, they combine mathematical and moral thinking. When a citizen evaluates a news story, they draw on historical, logical, and ethical thought.

Understanding the kinds of thinking gives you tools to choose the right one for the moment. A hammer cannot solve every problem; neither can emotion or instinct. But knowing when to analyze, when to question, and when simply to observe turns the mind into a complete instrument.

Critical Thinking

Critical Thinking is disciplined, deliberate, and aimed at truth. It doesn't settle for what seems right; it asks *why* it seems right and *whether* it truly is. It is the mind's immune system, filtering out falsehood and sharpening judgment.

Michael Scriven and Richard Paul defined it as "the intellectually disciplined process of actively and skillfully conceptualizing, applying, analyzing, synthesizing, and evaluating information..." The key word is *disciplined*. Everyday thought drifts like wind, but critical thought walks a chosen path, guided by logic, evidence, and fairness.

Consider Abraham Lincoln writing the Emancipation Proclamation. He weighed morality against law, strategy against timing, conviction against consequence. That long inner debate, between emotion and reason, was the work of critical thinking.

Core Skills of Critical Thinking

1. **Interpretation** – Comprehend what is actually being said or shown, not what you wish it meant. A scientist interprets data; a teacher interprets behavior. Misinterpretation is the root of most human conflict.
2. **Finding Meaning** – Go beyond surface facts to uncover significance. Reading statistics without context is arithmetic; connecting them to human impact is understanding.
3. **Analysis** – Break ideas into parts and study their connections. Why did a plan fail? Which assumption collapsed first? Analysis prevents superstition by tracing cause and effect.
4. **Inference** – Draw sound conclusions from limited data. A detective who sees footprints in wet soil and infers direction is practicing everyday logic.
5. **Evaluation** – Judge credibility and relevance. In the digital age, this means checking sources and motives before believing a headline.
6. **Explanation** – Present conclusions clearly enough for others to test. If you cannot explain it simply, you probably don't yet understand it.
7. **Self-Regulation** – Observe your own thinking while you think. It's the mental equivalent of proofreading your sentences as you write them.

Scheffer and Rubenfeld added:

8. **Application of Logic** – Ensuring each statement follows naturally from the previous one.
9. **Interrogation** – Asking questions that pierce appearance to reach essence. Socrates used this so effectively that "Socratic dialogue" remains the model for education.
10. **Discrimination** – Telling signal from noise, an ability that separates a genius from a crank.

To these we can add:

11. **Elaborating** – Expanding an idea into new territory. Many discoveries, Velcro, X-rays, microwave ovens, came from minds that asked, "What else could this do?"
12. **Debating** – Testing ideas in the open, where logic replaces volume. A true debate seeks clarity, not conquest.
13. **Transforming** – Recasting a thought into another form. A poet turns grief into verse; an engineer turns friction into propulsion.
14. **Anticipating** – Imagining outcomes before they happen, so choice precedes crisis.

Critical Thinking is less about intelligence than intention. It demands honesty about bias, courage to admit ignorance, and patience to follow reason where it leads. It means pausing before reacting, separating evidence from emotion, and remembering that conviction is not proof.

Developing this discipline takes practice. Read authors who challenge you, not only those who agree. Rephrase complex ideas aloud until they make sense in plain language. Question the reliability of every "obvious" claim, including your own.

In a society flooded with opinion and outrage, Critical Thinking is civic armor. It protects democracy from manipulation and the individual from error.

Interrogatory Thinking

If Critical Thinking is the art of judgment, Interrogatory Thinking is its engine; it begins with a question. The right question can move mountains of ignorance; the wrong one can bury truth beneath assumption.

Carl Sagan called questions "the sharp tools of discovery." Children use them instinctively, asking *why* a thousand times a day until adults teach them to stop. Restoring that curiosity is the first step toward real intellect.

Asking good questions requires three disciplines: curiosity, precision, and empathy.

- **Curiosity** drives the need to know. "What else might be true?" keeps the mind alive.
- **Precision** shapes questions so they uncover, not confuse. "How does this work?" is stronger than "Why is this bad?"
- **Empathy** ensures tone invites answers instead of defensiveness. The goal is illumination, not victory.

In leadership, the quality of questions often defines success. A manager who asks, "What obstacles prevent you from succeeding?" learns more than one who asks, "Why aren't you performing?" The first seeks understanding; the second assigns blame.

Jim Camp, in *The Science of Asking Great Questions,* emphasized that phrasing is persuasion. Questions beginning with *what* or *how* encourage reflection, whereas *can* or *is* often produce yes-or-no walls.

Framing also matters. Setting context, why you ask, how the answer will help, builds trust. When people sense respect, they reveal truth.

At its highest level, Interrogatory Thinking turns inward. "What am I avoiding?" "Why do I believe this?" Those questions dissolve ego's armor and make growth possible.

Logical Thinking

Logical Thinking is structure applied to thought, the skeleton that gives reasoning its shape. Where Critical Thinking tests ideas, Logical Thinking connects them.

Roger Sperry's split-brain research showed that the left hemisphere manages sequence, language, and analysis, the *chattering mind* that organizes chaos into order. Without it, the right brain's imagination would wander endlessly.

The left side:

- Governs the right side of the body and right visual field.
- Processes input sequentially and analytically.
- Notices parts before wholes.
- Measures time, constructs sentences, and plans tasks.
- Is the seat of reasoning, mathematics, and verbal skill.

But logic alone is not wisdom; it is precision without compassion. A balanced thinker uses logic to build, not to bludgeon.

The Steps of Logical Thinking

1. **Define the Goal.** Be specific. "Increase sales" is wishful; "Increase quarterly revenue by 10 percent through new customer referrals" is a goal. The clearer the destination, the straighter the path.
2. **Plan Systematically.** Break the goal into steps. Engineers call this *design thinking*; philosophers call it *method.*
3. **Use Information.** Facts are the bricks of logic. Gather, sort, and verify them. Incomplete data is like missing pieces in a puzzle, forcing the mind to guess and often to err.
4. **Reason.** Link each step to the next through evidence. If the connection is weak, strengthen it or discard it. Reasoning is the mental equivalent of structural testing.
5. **Validate.** Test conclusions by comparison with experience, expert review, or repetition. Science calls this *replication*; everyday life calls it *double-checking your work.*

Logical Thinking underlies every serious pursuit, from law to architecture, from chess to computer programming. A programmer debugging code follows pure logic: if A and B produce error C, trace back to see which assumption failed. The same habit serves a parent deciding rules for a teenager or a voter weighing competing claims.

Logic also has forms:

- **Analytic Thinking**, dividing a problem into smaller parts.
- **Deductive Reasoning**, moving from general rule to specific instance ("All metals expand when heated; iron is metal; therefore iron expands").

- **Inductive Reasoning**, moving from observed specifics to general rule ("The sun has risen every day; it will rise tomorrow").
- **Abductive Reasoning**, inferring the most likely cause from incomplete evidence (used by doctors and detectives).
- **Backward Reasoning**, starting from a desired result and tracing the steps required to reach it.

Each form serves different ends. The scientist favors induction, the mathematician deduction, the detective abduction. A skilled thinker shifts among them as a carpenter changes tools.

Logical Thinking demands humility. The instant you assume you cannot be wrong, you stop being logical. True reasoning holds doubt as a companion, not an enemy.

Scientific Thinking

Scientific Thinking is disciplined curiosity, an organized attempt to understand the world through observation, evidence, and testing. Its purpose is not to prove what we wish were true but to discover what *is* true, even when it contradicts our hopes.

Science progresses by moving from the known to the unknown, from question to hypothesis, from hypothesis to experiment, and from experiment to conclusion. Each step invites doubt. The strength of science lies not in certainty but in its willingness to challenge its own conclusions.

Galileo used the telescope to prove that the heavens were not immutable spheres but moving bodies; Darwin used field observation to show that species evolve; Marie Curie tested materials until she isolated radium. Each worked within the same pattern, observe, test, record, repeat.

At its core, scientific thinking requires two virtues: **patience** and **honesty.** Patience to follow the process wherever it leads; honesty to report results exactly as they occur. These virtues apply beyond laboratories, to business, politics, education, and daily life. Anyone can use the scientific mindset: identify a problem, propose possible causes, test them, and keep what works.

Steps in Scientific Thinking

1. **Observe.** Look closely, without judgment. A scientist notices details others ignore.
2. **Compare.** Find relationships between what is observed. Similarities and differences often reveal hidden principles.
3. **Sort and Organize.** Arrange facts so they can be analyzed; chaos hides meaning.
4. **Predict.** Use prior knowledge to anticipate outcomes. Every good forecast is a miniature hypothesis.
5. **Experiment.** Try, fail, adjust, and try again. Repetition exposes truth.
6. **Evaluate.** Examine results honestly, welcome criticism, and refine methods.
7. **Apply.** Extend what you have learned to new situations; knowledge that remains unused decays.

Scientific Thinking reminds us that facts are provisional. Today's truth is tomorrow's hypothesis. What endures is not any single conclusion but the discipline of continual testing.

Mathematical Thinking

Mathematical Thinking is the language of order and relationship. It gives structure to the universe and precision to thought.

To the uninitiated, mathematics appears rigid and mechanical; to those who practice it, it is imagination disciplined by logic. A mathematician visualizes patterns as an artist sees form. Numbers are not dry symbols, they are models of harmony.

Mathematical thinking teaches clarity. To solve a problem, you must first state it precisely. Vague questions yield vague answers. A clear equation is a clear thought.

This habit of exactness has broad application. In budgeting, design, engineering, even in argument, quantitative thinking brings proportion and balance. It forces you to separate fact from opinion: *How much? How often? By what ratio?*

Mathematics also develops humility. Each proof stands only until a counterexample is found. Accepting that principle trains the ego to yield to evidence. The same mindset that checks a formula should also check a belief.

Finally, mathematical thought nurtures creativity. Discovering a new proof or algorithm resembles composing music: both demand intuition, rhythm, and an appreciation of elegance.

Intuitive Thinking

Intuition is insight without conscious reasoning, a bridge between the known and the unknown. It is the subconscious drawing conclusions faster than logic can explain them.

Experienced minds rely on intuition constantly. A chess master "feels" the best move; a nurse senses a patient's condition before instruments confirm it; a seasoned investor reads market mood without charts. These are not miracles, but the result of pattern memory stored through long practice.

However, intuition can deceive when detached from experience. A novice driver who "feels" safe speeding in rain is not guided by intuition but ignorance. The reliability of intuition depends on the depth of the mind that produces it.

Strengthening Intuition

1. **Feed it knowledge.** Intuition works with stored material; the more you learn, the better it performs.
2. **Listen in stillness.** The subconscious speaks softly; noise drowns it out.
3. **Test its accuracy.** Compare intuitive impressions with actual results; keep score.
4. **Respect emotion, but verify it.** Feelings can guide but also mislead.

Plato wrote that the rational and the passionate mind must align before wisdom appears. When intellect and intuition cooperate, decisions gain both accuracy and humanity.

Emotion shapes intuition strongly. Fear narrows it, compassion broadens it. A surgeon must quiet fear to operate well; an artist must let feeling flow to create truth. The challenge is balance, reason steering emotion, emotion energizing reason.

In moments of crisis, intuition often acts before thought. A driver swerves; a parent catches a falling child. These instantaneous choices emerge from layers of training. The goal, therefore, is not to suppress intuition but to educate it; so that when instinct acts, it acts wisely.

Metacognition – Thinking About Thinking

Metacognition is the awareness of one's own thought process, the mind watching itself work. It is reflection raised to a higher power. Where reflection looks back, metacognition observes in real time.

Psychologists describe metacognition as the difference between *being inside a storm* and *watching the weather.* You are still in the same system, but you can now see the patterns forming.

Developing metacognition means learning to pause mid-thought and ask:

- *What am I assuming?*
- *What evidence supports this belief?*
- *Is my emotion steering my logic?*
- *Have I considered alternatives?*

This habit prevents automatic thinking, the kind that repeats old errors out of comfort or fear.

The Three Levels of Metacognition

1. **Awareness:** Recognizing what kind of thinking you are using, analytical, intuitive, emotional, or reactive.
2. **Control:** Adjusting your strategy when you realize it isn't working. A writer who shifts from editing to free-writing mid-block is practicing control.
3. **Evaluation:** Reviewing how well your thinking served its purpose. Did you reach a sound conclusion or merely a convenient one?

Metacognitive thinkers become efficient learners. They know when they understand and when they don't, when to ask for help, and when to persist. In leadership, this translates to clarity and humility, the ability to admit, "I may be wrong; let me re-examine."

Cultivating metacognition transforms intelligence into wisdom. It creates thinkers who not only reason but also *know how they reason.*

Curiosity and Creativity

Curiosity and creativity are twin forces: curiosity seeks the unknown; creativity brings it to life. Without curiosity, creativity starves. Without creativity, curiosity ends in trivia.

Curiosity is the mind reaching outward, driven by wonder. Every major leap in civilization began with a question: *What is beyond that ocean? What makes lightning strike? Why do apples fall downward?*

Todd Kashdan called curiosity "the desire to know or learn something." It flourishes in uncertainty. The thrill of discovery, not the possession of facts, fuels progress. People who embrace novelty, who take new routes, try new skills, meet new minds, age more slowly in thought and often in spirit.

Curiosity thrives when failure is safe. In schools and workplaces that punish mistakes, curiosity withers. But in environments that reward exploration, questions multiply and innovation follows.

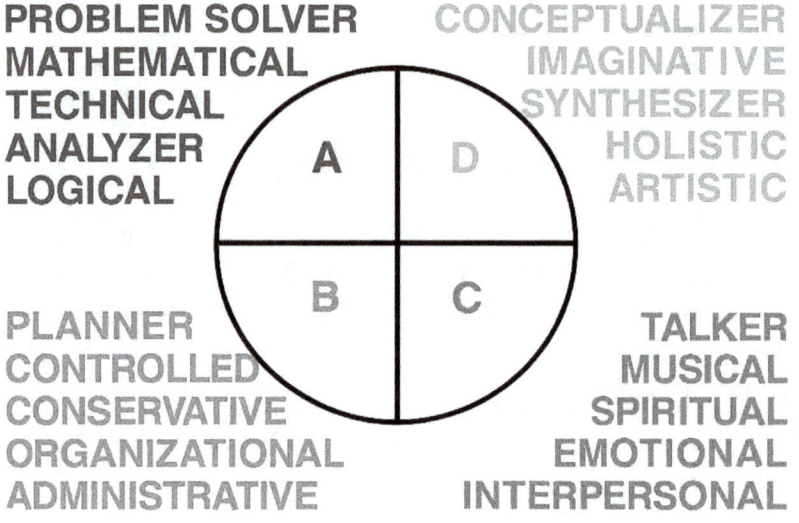

PROBLEM SOLVER   CONCEPTUALIZER
MATHEMATICAL   IMAGINATIVE
TECHNICAL   SYNTHESIZER
ANALYZER   HOLISTIC
LOGICAL   ARTISTIC

A   D   B   C

PLANNER   TALKER
CONTROLLED   MUSICAL
CONSERVATIVE   SPIRITUAL
ORGANIZATIONAL   EMOTIONAL
ADMINISTRATIVE   INTERPERSONAL

Creativity converts that curiosity into form. It is not limited to art; it is evident in engineering, teaching, cooking, problem-solving, any act that produces something new and useful.

Edward de Bono's concept of **Lateral Thinking** describes this process: looking sideways at a problem instead of head-on. A lateral thinker asks, "What if we reversed the roles?" or "What if we removed the rule everyone assumes?" Many breakthroughs, Post-it Notes, penicillin, even the safety glass in windshields, came from such detours.

Conditions for Creativity

1. **Freedom:** Space to experiment without immediate judgment.
2. **Diversity:** Exposure to different fields and viewpoints.
3. **Constraint:** Oddly enough, limits can spark creativity by forcing novel combinations.
4. **Play:** Unstructured exploration stimulates unexpected connections.

Creativity is not a flash of genius but a discipline of exploration. Thomas Edison performed thousands of failed experiments before finding a workable filament. Each "failure" was data.

Equally, creativity demands perseverance. Many abandon ideas after early setbacks, mistaking friction for impossibility. Yet most innovations emerge only after repeated refinement.

To cultivate creativity, schedule solitude and conversation in equal measure. Solitude lets ideas gestate; conversation lets them evolve. Keep a notebook, sketchbook, or voice recorder handy; inspiration rarely visits on command.

Finally, creativity must serve. The goal is not novelty for its own sake but improvement, for beauty, usefulness, or understanding. True creative thinking enriches others as well as the thinker.

The Interplay of Thought

All forms of thinking, logical, scientific, intuitive, reflective, and creative, interact continuously. Logic tests intuition; intuition humanizes logic. Reflection refines experience; metacognition governs them all.

Thinking is not merely an academic pursuit. It is how we shape our lives, our societies, and our future. To think well is to live deliberately, to choose clarity over confusion, patience over impulse, truth over comfort.

Every improvement in the human story, from fire to flight, from poetry to physics, began with someone who dared to think a little longer, a little deeper, and a little differently.

Thinking, in all its forms, is the foundation of awareness and action. It is how we translate perception into understanding and imagination into reality. Yet even the most disciplined thinking must rest upon something deeper, our capacity to *know*, to *interpret*, and to *apply* what we have learned. Intelligence refines that capacity, knowledge sustains it, and common sense grounds it in the realities of everyday life. To think well is valuable; to think wisely is essential. In the next chapter, we'll explore how intelligence, knowledge, and common sense work together to transform thought into effective action, the bridge between mental skill and real-world success.

Chapter 3: Intelligence, Knowledge, and Common Sense

Understanding the distinctions between being smart, knowledgeable, having common sense, and possessing intelligence is crucial for recognizing different cognitive strengths and how they shape decision-making. Each of these attributes contributes uniquely to how we interpret reality, approach challenges, and adapt to change.

A complete thinker does not rely on one form of mental ability but combines several, logic with intuition, intellect with empathy, knowledge with humility. Throughout history, it is not the most educated or even the most intelligent individuals who have most improved the human condition, but those who learned to balance thought with judgment and principle with practicality.

To think well is to see clearly, but to live well requires applying that clarity to the complex, unpredictable flow of life. This chapter examines how different forms of understanding, smartness, knowledge, common sense, and intelligence, overlap, diverge, and ultimately complete one another.

Being Smart

Being smart is not a single gift but a coordinated set of mental skills. It reflects both quickness of thought and soundness of judgment, a blend of alertness, adaptability, and self-awareness.

In daily life, we recognize smartness intuitively. It's the coworker who solves problems before others realize they exist, the friend who can diffuse tension with a perfectly timed comment, or the leader who anticipates challenges and adjusts course before the storm hits.

Let's explore its core elements in depth.

1. **Quick-Wittedness:**
   Quick-wittedness is the ability to think on your feet and respond effectively to unexpected change. It is not simply speed of thought, but relevance of response. In conversation, it might mean answering a difficult question with insight rather than defensiveness. In a crisis, it means acting decisively when hesitation could make things worse. Quick-witted individuals can improvise solutions in real time because they trust their trained instincts.

2. **Sharpness:**
   Sharpness combines insight and discrimination. It's the knack for seeing what others overlook, the small inconsistency in an argument, the subtle cue in someone's tone, the opportunity hiding inside a problem. A sharp mind cuts through complexity the way a honed blade cuts through rope: cleanly and efficiently.

3. **Mental Alertness:**
   Alertness is constant readiness of mind. It keeps attention awake even when the body is tired. Mentally alert people catch nuances others miss; they sense when a conversation shifts, when someone's motives change, or when a decision begins to drift off course. Alertness is not anxiety, it is awareness without panic, presence without overreaction.

4. **Knowledge Combined with Logical Thinking:**
   Knowledge alone is static, but when paired with logic it becomes dynamic. A smart person applies facts flexibly, connecting ideas across contexts. For example, an entrepreneur might apply lessons from biology, adaptation, and evolution to business strategy,

recognizing that survival favors the nimble, not the large.

5. **Shrewdness (with Integrity):**
   True shrewdness is strategic intelligence, the ability to see consequences before they arrive. A shrewd diplomat, for instance, balances risk and reward, anticipating human behavior rather than manipulating it. The difference between shrewdness and cunning lies in motive: shrewdness seeks advantage through wisdom; cunning seeks it through deceit.

6. **Ethical Awareness:**
   Being smart includes the capacity to use intellect responsibly. History is filled with brilliant manipulators whose cleverness caused harm. The truly smart mind understands that ethics is not a constraint on intelligence but its compass.

7. **Discernment of Truth:**
   Perhaps the highest form of smartness is the ability to separate truth from illusion. In an age of misinformation, this skill matters more than ever. The smart person resists the temptation of easy answers and looks for consistency, evidence, and integrity behind every claim.

Together, these qualities make smartness a form of applied intelligence, a practical combination of speed, precision, and ethics.

Being Knowledgeable

Knowledge is often confused with information, but it is not the same. Information is a collection of facts; knowledge is understanding those facts within context. It is what transforms data into meaning.

A knowledgeable person sees not only what *is* but *why it matters*. This deeper understanding gives them confidence without arrogance. They recognize patterns and consequences across fields, allowing them to make better judgments in both professional and personal life.

1. **Intelligent Understanding:**
   Knowledge involves the ability to connect ideas across domains. For example, a historian who studies economic patterns understands that revolutions often follow shortages; a physician who studies psychology understands that healing requires both medicine and belief. This cross-connection between disciplines is the seed of wisdom.

2. **Being Well-Informed:**
   A knowledgeable person keeps up with developments in multiple fields. They read widely, listen critically, and avoid the trap of confirmation bias. Being well-informed is not about memorizing news headlines, it's about understanding how today's events echo past ones and forecast future possibilities.

3. **Subject-Matter Expertise:**
   Depth complements breadth. Whether you are a teacher, scientist, craftsman, or artist, expertise in one domain allows you to contribute meaningfully to others. It's through mastery that creativity flourishes; Leonardo da Vinci's genius arose not from dabbling, but from deep study in anatomy, geometry, and mechanics.

4. **Fundamental Understanding Across Disciplines:**
   The most insightful thinkers are generalists at heart. They may specialize, but they never stop learning outside their field. They understand enough about economics to manage their money, enough about psychology to lead others, and enough about history to avoid repeating it. The Renaissance ideal, the "well-rounded mind," remains as valuable today as ever.

5. **Historical Insight:**
   History is knowledge tested by time. A knowledgeable person studies the past not to memorize dates but to

understand cause and consequence. Knowing why empires collapsed or reforms succeeded provides a map for the present. As the philosopher George Santayana warned, "Those who cannot remember the past are condemned to repeat it."

A knowledgeable mind becomes a compass for navigating uncertainty. It balances memory with imagination and principle with pragmatism. Without that balance, knowledge can become trivia, impressive but inert.

In the age of artificial intelligence and digital overload, knowledge is no longer about access but interpretation. Machines can store and retrieve data; only humans can understand meaning.

Common Sense: Often Overlooked Intelligence

Common sense is intelligence distilled through experience. It is how the mind translates knowledge into survival and decency. While intelligence analyzes complexity, common sense simplifies it.

It's the quiet voice that says, "That may be legal, but it's not wise," or "That may be true in theory, but it won't work here." It's what allows a mechanic, a nurse, or a parent to make better decisions than a scholar who knows everything except what matters most.

Common sense is the meeting point of observation, intuition, reasoning, and empathy.

Components of Common Sense

1. **Observation:**
   Common sense begins with seeing clearly. You cannot interpret what you have not noticed. People with strong observational skills recognize subtle cues: tone of voice, posture, weather patterns, timing, or unspoken moods. Observation grounds thinking in reality.
2. **Intuition:**
   Intuition allows quick recognition of patterns from experience. It is not mysticism, it's memory operating at high speed. A firefighter senses when a structure is unsafe not because of luck, but because thousands of past experiences whisper "something's wrong."
3. **Reasoning:**
   Common sense depends on reasoning to test intuition. It keeps emotion in check by asking, "Does this make sense?" or "What evidence supports this?" Reasoning turns instinct into judgment.
4. **Empathy:**
   Empathy gives common sense its humanity. Without it, decisions may be efficient but heartless. Understanding others' feelings and motives prevents unnecessary conflict and leads to wiser compromises.

Developing Common Sense

Although often described as "natural," common sense is cultivated through attention and humility.

- **Experience:** Exposure to varied situations trains the mind to recognize cause and effect. The person who learns from mistakes, rather than resenting them, doubles their wisdom each time.
- **Critical Thinking:** Engage with puzzles, dilemmas, and debates. Testing your reasoning sharpens practical logic.

- **Learning from Others:** Observe the judgment of people who consistently make good decisions, mentors, elders, or skilled colleagues. Notice *how* they think, not just *what* they decide.
- **Reflection:** After acting, review outcomes honestly. What worked? What didn't? Reflection converts experience into usable wisdom.

Common sense may appear simple, but it is the rarest of intelligences. In a world obsessed with credentials and complexity, common sense remains the quality most essential for trust, leadership, and personal peace. It balances intellect with practicality and grounds human brilliance in reality.

In essence, common sense is the mind's internal governor. It prevents brilliance from turning reckless and intelligence from turning cold. Without it, the smartest person may still act foolishly; with it, even an ordinary mind can achieve extraordinary stability.

Understanding Intelligence

Intelligence is among the most studied yet misunderstood human capacities. It is not a single measurable trait, like height or weight, but a living system of abilities that interact dynamically. Intelligence allows us to learn, reason, plan, solve problems, understand abstract ideas, and adapt to changing environments.

Contrary to popular belief, intelligence is not confined to IQ or academic performance. It includes emotional sensitivity, adaptability, self-awareness, and moral judgment, traits that cannot be fully captured by tests. A person may score high on logic puzzles yet fail to manage their own impulses; another may lack formal education but consistently make wise and timely decisions.

Truly intelligent people use both sides of their mind: the analytical and the intuitive, the rational and the emotional. They not only process information, they *interpret* it, discern what matters, and act on it wisely.

Below are the foundational elements that collectively define intelligence.

1. **Ability to Learn and Understand:**
   Learning is the seed of all intelligence. The capacity to grasp new ideas, connect them with past knowledge, and apply them flexibly defines mental agility. For instance, a person who learns a new language not only memorizes vocabulary but also begins to sense rhythm, tone, and culture, a broader understanding that extends beyond words.

2. **Distinguishing Between Fact, Fiction, and Fantasy:**
   Intelligence requires discernment, the ability to separate what is demonstrably true from what merely feels true. This skill protects against manipulation, propaganda, and wishful thinking. In an era of misinformation, intellectual vigilance has become a moral duty.

3. **Awareness of Meaning:**
   To be intelligent is to perceive depth. Two people may read the same story: one sees entertainment, the other sees a parable of human behavior. Awareness of meaning turns raw knowledge into insight.

4. **Knowledge of What Is True or False:**
   This arises from combining historical understanding, reasoning, and instinct. The intelligent mind triangulates truth by asking, "What happened before? What evidence exists now? What does experience suggest?"

5. **Use of Reason and Logical Thinking:**
   Reason organizes thought into coherent form. It allows the mind to separate emotional impulse from factual evaluation. Intelligent reasoning doesn't reject emotion,

it puts it in proportion, giving the heart a voice without letting it seize the microphone.

6. **Abstract Thinking:**
Abstract thought is the engine of creativity and invention. It allows us to imagine what does not yet exist, to see the invisible structure behind visible reality. Einstein's theory of relativity began not with formulas, but with a thought experiment: imagining himself riding a beam of light.

7. **Mental Acuteness:**
Sharpness of thought enables swift comprehension and decisive action. It's the ability to grasp essence without getting lost in detail, to "see through" problems rather than around them. A mentally acute person hears both what is said and what is left unsaid.

8. **Connecting Disparate Concepts:**
The most powerful sign of intelligence is synthesis, the ability to combine seemingly unrelated ideas into new frameworks. Innovation often arises from cross-pollination: physics inspiring philosophy, art informing technology, biology influencing design.

Intelligence thrives where curiosity meets courage. It asks, *"What if?"* and then dares to find out.

Assessing your own intelligence doesn't require a test, it requires reflection. Which of these abilities comes naturally? Which can be improved? Intelligence grows through awareness of its own limits. Once you see where your mind falters, growth begins.

Brilliance versus Genius

The Essence of Brilliance

Brilliance is concentrated light, sharp, dazzling, and immediate. It reflects quick comprehension, originality, and clarity of expression. Brilliant individuals illuminate problems so others can see them plainly.

1. **Confidence and Presence:**
   True brilliance radiates quiet confidence rather than arrogance. It's the calm assurance that comes from mastery. Florence Nightingale revolutionized hospital sanitation not through self-promotion, but through firm conviction backed by evidence. Confidence grounded in competence inspires trust.
2. **Clarity and Precision:**
   Brilliant thinkers can distill complexity into clarity. They translate the abstract into the understandable. When Carl Sagan said, "We are made of star stuff," he compressed a universe of astrophysics into a sentence anyone could grasp.
3. **Adaptability and Versatility:**
   Brilliance is agile. It thrives under change. A brilliant leader recognizes when a plan has outlived its usefulness and pivots with grace. Adaptability is the mark of flexible intelligence, unafraid to update itself.
4. **Vision and Insight:**
   Brilliant individuals see beyond the obvious. They notice patterns before others do and imagine possibilities that others find improbable. Steve Jobs's vision of personal computing was not prediction, it was perception sharpened by imagination.
5. **Influence and Impact:**
   Brilliance has ripple effects. It changes how others think, often redefining an entire field. But brilliance

without integrity can become destructive; influence must serve progress, not ego.

Brilliance is rare but cultivable. It grows in the soil of focus, practice, and self-questioning. Every time you simplify a complex problem or communicate an idea clearly, you practice the craft of brilliance.

Genius

If brilliance is lightning, genius is the storm that generates it. Genius extends beyond intelligence or creativity, it is sustained originality that transforms the world.

National Geographic once described genius as "a passion for curiosity." That is true, but incomplete. Curiosity ignites the spark; discipline keeps it burning. Genius marries restless wonder with unrelenting effort.

1. **Curiosity as Catalyst:**
   Genius begins with curiosity, an unquenchable drive to understand. Leonardo da Vinci dissected corpses not out of morbidity, but to grasp the mechanics of life. Marie Curie endured radiation sickness to reveal the secrets of atoms. Their curiosity was not idle, it was purposeful exploration.
2. **Achievement as Definition:**
   Society recognizes genius through results. The word carries meaning only when linked to achievement that alters understanding or capability. Alfred Nobel's transformation from arms inventor to patron of peace demonstrates that genius includes moral awakening as well as intellect.
3. **Preparedness and Opportunity:**
   Louis Pasteur observed that "chance favors the prepared mind." Genius does not wait for inspiration, it builds the capacity to recognize it when it arrives. The so-called

"Aha! moment" is rarely sudden; it is the visible crest of a long, invisible climb.

4. **Resilience and Perseverance:**
   Most geniuses fail more often than they succeed. What distinguishes them is persistence through uncertainty. Thomas Edison reportedly said, "I have not failed. I've just found 10,000 ways that won't work." Genius transforms failure into fuel.

5. **Environment and Association:**
   Genius thrives among other inquiring minds. The conversations at the cafés of Paris during the Enlightenment or the salons of Vienna in the 19th century generated entire movements of thought. The company you keep shapes the horizons you see.

6. **Education and Depth:**
   Modern education often prizes breadth over depth. Yet genius demands the opposite, deep immersion. To master a field, the mind must dwell in it long enough to see its invisible structure. A slower, more contemplative form of education might produce fewer test scores but more breakthroughs.

7. **The Age of Genius:**
   While certain ages favor productivity, genius is not bound by time. Grandma Moses began painting in her seventies; Einstein made breakthroughs in his thirties. What matters is intensity of focus, not youth or age.

8. **Genius and Humility:**
   Paradoxically, most geniuses are humble before the mystery of existence. They know that what they have discovered is a fragment of a much larger truth. They live in awe, not arrogance.

The Paradox of Genius

Society often admires genius yet resists it. Genius challenges convention and disturbs comfort. Ernest Dimnet noted that people admire great minds but also feel diminished by them. The irony is that every act of genius expands, rather than threatens, human possibility.

Genius, at its heart, is not about superiority, it's about service. The true genius gives humanity new tools, new beauty, or new understanding. The light it sheds is not meant to blind but to guide.

Intelligence, knowledge, and common sense are not separate peaks but connected ridges on the same mountain of awareness. Each strengthens the other: intelligence gives structure, knowledge gives substance, and common sense gives grounding. Brilliance and genius rise higher still, not by abandoning those foundations but by perfecting them.

The complete thinker cultivates all of these dimensions, not to become extraordinary, but to live and act with extraordinary effectiveness.

To understand the mind is to understand its responsibility. Every act of thought shapes reality, our choices, our communities, and the world that inherits them.

The mind is a living system, shaped not only by intelligence, knowledge, and common sense but also by the many forces that influence how we think. Our upbringing, emotions, environment, habits, and even the information we consume all play a role in directing or distorting our thoughts. Understanding these influences is as important as mastering the art of thinking itself. In the next chapter, we'll explore the factors that shape thought, those that strengthen it, those that weaken it, and how awareness of these forces can help you take greater control of your own mind.

Chapter 4: Factors Affecting Thought

Our thoughts do not exist in isolation. They are constantly shaped, disrupted, and redirected by countless influences, some external, some internal, some fleeting, and others deeply ingrained. To understand how to think better, we must first understand what affects thinking itself. Confidence, environment, fatigue, emotion, distraction, and even the information we choose to consume can either sharpen or cloud the mind. Recognizing these forces gives us the power to master them.

Confidence and Its Fluctuations

Confidence is not a constant; it rises and falls like a tide, influenced by our experiences, relationships, and beliefs about ourselves. Most people feel self-doubt more often than self-assurance, especially when facing uncertainty or criticism. Yet this mental balance determines whether thought is bold or timid, constructive or defensive.

When confidence wanes, thinking becomes reactive. We second-guess decisions, replay failures, and interpret neutral events as threats. The mind, once clear, becomes crowded with hesitation. But when confidence is high, thought flows freely. We make connections faster, articulate ideas better, and see possibilities instead of barriers.

True confidence comes from competence and reflection, not ego. It grows through experience, successes that reinforce ability and failures that reveal resilience. You can build confidence in your thinking by keeping a record of insights that proved correct, or by revisiting challenges you once solved.

Each reminder strengthens the belief that your mind is capable and trustworthy.

Consider the architect who hesitated early in his career, questioning every line on the page. Over time, experience taught him which instincts to trust and which to question. By his tenth project, he no longer doubted every decision, his confidence had become quiet but unshakable. The same process occurs in thought: repetition, correction, and persistence build assurance.

The key is balance. Overconfidence blinds you to error; underconfidence blinds you to opportunity. Thought functions best when humility and assurance coexist.

Mastering Distractions

Distractions are the great thieves of thought. In a world of notifications, noise, and endless scrolling, attention has become a scarce resource. Yet deep thinking requires stillness, a protected space in which ideas can mature.

Controlling distraction begins with awareness. Notice what consistently interrupts your concentration. Is it sound, stress, boredom, or habit? Each cause demands a different response. For sound, seek quiet; for stress, pause and breathe; for boredom, refresh your curiosity.

Relaxation often leads to deeper insight because a calm mind can wander creatively without scattering. Conversely, intense focus is required when clarity matters most, writing, designing, solving, deciding. The thinker must learn to shift gears: tension for precision, calm for imagination.

Consider the scientist in a noisy lab. She learns to ignore the clatter of instruments, but when she steps outside for a quiet walk, the solution she needed surfaces effortlessly. The lesson is not that noise kills thought, but that different kinds of thought require different kinds of silence.

Enjoyable activities, music, gardening, walking, can create a rhythm that steadies thought. They quiet surface chatter, allowing deeper ideas to surface. Even routine chores can become gateways to concentration if done with awareness.

Creating the Right Environment

Your surroundings influence your mental state more than most realize. Noise, clutter, and disorganization compete for attention; order and calm promote reflection. A quiet, comfortable space signals to the brain that it is time to focus.

If possible, choose a location free from interruption. If not, create boundaries: silence your phone, close unnecessary tabs, and inform others of your thinking time. Environmental discipline fosters mental discipline.

Physical comfort matters, too. A fatigued or tense body breeds restless thoughts. Take breaks to move, stretch, or breathe deeply. Hydration and posture also affect mental clarity. A well-rested mind in a well-prepared setting becomes far more efficient.

When fatigue or distraction persists, step away briefly. Many great thinkers, from Darwin to Einstein, relied on walking as part of their creative process. Darwin's "thinking path" behind his home in Kent became a physical ritual for intellectual renewal. Movement rebalances attention, clearing the mind for fresh insight.

Addressing Mental Fatigue and Boredom

Fatigue dulls perception. It narrows thought to the immediate and the obvious. When the mind is tired, even small decisions seem heavy. Rest, nutrition, and varied activity restore the brain's rhythm.

Boredom, however, is not fatigue, it is the absence of engagement. A bored mind turns inward, seeking stimulation, often in unproductive ways. The remedy is curiosity. Direct attention toward questions or topics that spark wonder. Curiosity awakens energy, and energy renews focus.

If your work or studies feel stale, reframe them. Ask, "What about this haven't I noticed before?" or "How would someone from another field approach this?" Fresh angles revive old interest. A shift in viewpoint can reignite mental fire.

An engineer once told me he overcame creative blocks by keeping a notebook labeled "Unrelated Ideas." Whenever he was stuck, he flipped through pages of strange observations, most useless, a few brilliant. It wasn't the notes that mattered but the act of opening the door to curiosity.

Thoughts and Feelings

Thoughts are not feelings, but they interact constantly. Thoughts can trigger emotions, and emotions can inspire or distort thoughts. Fear, anger, or excitement alters perception, changing what the mind notices and how it interprets events.

Emotion is faster than intellect, it reacts before reason can intervene. That is why people often say how they feel when asked what they think, and vice versa. The two languages share a grammar. A calm emotional state enables clear reasoning; a turbulent one floods logic with bias.

To think well, acknowledge your emotions without surrendering to them. Name them, observe them, and let them settle. The mind cannot see through stormy waters.

A manager facing criticism once practiced this skill deliberately. Before replying to a harsh email, he waited an hour, reread it calmly, and found his anger had faded. His eventual response was concise and professional, proof that cooling emotion improves thought.

Connecting Emotion and Interest

People think most deeply about what they care about. Engage someone emotionally, and their mind follows. A teacher who inspires curiosity does more than transfer knowledge, he awakens thought. Likewise, when you connect ideas to your own passions or experiences, thinking becomes effortless and enduring. Emotion is the spark; reasoning is the flame.

A musician learning harmony studies faster when analyzing favorite songs. Emotion provides a hook that memory clings to. Similarly, connecting study topics to your personal goals converts abstract information into meaningful understanding.

Ways to Think More Quickly

Mental agility can be trained. Lisa Mulcahy's "12 Ways to Think Faster" offers practical tools, but speed without depth is useless. The goal is not haste but responsiveness, thinking efficiently while retaining accuracy.

Among her suggestions:

1. **Decide Promptly.** Prolonged hesitation breeds confusion. Gather enough facts, then act. Reflection refines results later.
2. **Know Your Topic.** Broad reading expands comprehension, linking ideas across fields.
3. **Encourage Yourself.** Positive self-talk reinforces confidence and momentum.
4. **Clear Your Mind.** Movement: walking, driving, and stretching, resets cognition.
5. **Exercise.** Physical activity consolidates learning and boosts memory.
6. **Yawn.** Surprisingly, yawning cools the brain, improving efficiency.
7. **Improvise.** Activities like free writing or music improvisation stimulate creativity and rapid association.
8. **Read Literary Fiction.** Complex narratives enhance empathy and neural connectivity.
9. **Change Posture.** Alternate between sitting and standing to refresh attention.
10. **Chew Gum.** Simple motion increases blood flow and recall.
11. **Explore New Directions.** Curiosity strengthens adaptability.
12. **Maintain Brain Health.** Vitamin D and K2 support mental performance.

One executive applied these principles during morning commutes. Instead of scanning email, she dictated quick reflections on current challenges. By the time she arrived, her thoughts were sorted and sharper than after any meeting. Thinking faster begins with thinking healthier, mentally, physically, and emotionally.

Resisting the Pressure of Circumstances

When urgency rises, reason often retreats. Many people act under pressure without thinking, surrendering to fear or social momentum. In such moments, slogans replace thought and authority replaces judgment. The antidote is pause.

Before deciding, perform a brief internal check: What am I reacting to? Is this fear, fatigue, or fact? Write down pros and cons, even if hastily. Doing so slows emotion and invites reason back into the room.

If you seek advice, choose wisely. Consult those who have demonstrated good judgment, not merely confidence. And when you do, weigh their motives as carefully as their opinions. A decision made in calm reflection will outlast a dozen made in haste.

During crises, history's best leaders maintained composure by slowing down their thinking. Lincoln often read poetry before addressing matters of war. The rhythm and perspective restored calm logic where chaos tempted panic.

What Separates Top-Tier Minds

According to Neurohacker Collective, two variables distinguish exceptional thinkers: **what they learn** and **how effectively they learn it**. Both are within your control.

What you learn shapes your worldview; how you learn determines whether that knowledge becomes usable. Feed your mind material that challenges and refines your reasoning. Then reinforce learning through repetition, application, and reflection. The mind, like muscle, strengthens through deliberate effort.

Motivation fuels both processes. Interest and curiosity are mental accelerators, when you care about a subject, comprehension deepens and recall improves.

Consider two students: one memorizes facts for a test, the other explores the topic's connections to life and work. The first gains information; the second gains understanding. Top-tier minds chase meaning, not memory.

The Limits of Inspiration

Inspirational speeches can stir emotion but rarely create lasting change. Real transformation begins internally. Zig Ziglar's exercise illustrates this truth: Write down everything you wish you were doing or dream of doing. Then ask yourself, "Why can't I start now?" Often, the only barrier is permission, the willingness to believe it's possible. When thought changes, life follows.

A college student once told me she'd repeated Ziglar's exercise every January for five years. By the sixth, she realized half her list had already come true. She had not made resolutions; she had made a habit of thinking differently.

Deciding: The Architecture of Choice

Decision-making is organized thought in motion. Poor decisions usually come from haste, incomplete data, or ignoring experience. Good decisions follow a process:

1. **Clarify.** Define what decision truly needs to be made and what outcome you want.
2. **Collect Information.** Gather, sort, and summarize relevant facts.
3. **Consult.** Seek insight from those with expertise or perspective.

4. **Create Alternatives.** Brainstorm freely before judging ideas.
5. **Cull and Rank.** Remove weaker options and evaluate the remaining ones objectively.
6. **Choose and Commit.** Once made, act decisively. Doubt after decision is paralysis disguised as prudence.

Use tools like decision matrices or simple scoring systems when choices are complex. They replace emotion with structure.

Consider the NASA engineers of Apollo 13. Under extreme pressure, they saved the crew not through panic or luck, but by applying procedure and discipline. Structure became survival.

Reading as Mental Nutrition

Reading is one of the purest forms of mental exercise. It condenses lifetimes of experience into hours of engagement. What you read determines how you think.

Choose books that challenge and inspire rather than merely entertain. Quality reading doesn't just pass time, it expands perspective. The best books awaken questions, not answers. Read slowly enough to absorb, but briskly enough to sustain curiosity. Note passages that provoke reflection.

Strong readers are strong thinkers because they build inner libraries of reference and analogy. Every book you fully understand becomes part of your mind's vocabulary.

A business leader once summarized it this way: "Every great book I've read lets me think with a borrowed mind." Reading extends consciousness beyond the limits of personal experience.

Our thoughts, shaped by confidence, environment, fatigue, emotion, and discipline, define how clearly we see the world. To think well is not simply to possess intelligence, it is to manage these influences wisely. But what within us does the managing?

What are the qualities of the mind itself that make thinking possible? In the next chapter, we'll explore the **characteristics of the mind and the thinker**, the living engine that generates every thought, judgment, and insight you will ever have.

Chapter 5: Characteristics of the Mind and the Thinker

The human mind is both the tool and the craftsman of thought. It observes, reasons, imagines, and decides. It can rise to clarity or fall into confusion, depending on how it is directed. Understanding the nature of the mind is essential to mastering thought. The mind has specific traits, habits of perception, tendencies of focus, emotional filters, and biases that shape every conclusion we reach. Recognizing these traits does not weaken thought, it refines it.

The Mind as Observer

At its most basic level, the mind is an observer. It notices and records the flow of experience, including sights, sounds, sensations, emotions, and memories. But the mind is not a camera, it interprets what it sees. Every observation is colored by expectation and emotion.

Two people can witness the same event and come away with entirely different interpretations. One sees insult, another sees misunderstanding. This difference arises not from the event itself, but from the lens through which it was viewed. The observer shapes reality.

Consider a teacher watching a disruptive student. One teacher assumes disrespect, another sees insecurity. Each will act differently based on perception. Awareness of this bias allows a more accurate reading of reality. The skilled thinker recognizes when interpretation overshadows observation and pauses to ask, "What exactly did I see, and what did I add to it?"

Observation, then, is both a skill and a discipline. The more clearly we observe, the less we distort. Training the mind to separate perception from projection is one of the highest forms of intelligence.

The Mind as Interpreter

Observation collects raw data, interpretation assigns meaning. The human mind cannot resist connecting dots. We are natural storytellers, and we fill gaps with inference. This ability builds civilizations, and it can also start wars. It explains both art and superstition.

Interpretation is essential, yet it is also dangerous. It simplifies reality into patterns we can manage. The problem arises when those patterns become rigid. A thinker must remain flexible enough to revise interpretations when new evidence appears.

Imagine an archaeologist uncovering fragments of pottery. The first assumption might be that they belonged to a cooking vessel. Later discoveries suggest ritual use. A dogmatic thinker defends the first interpretation, an open mind adjusts it. Progress depends on mental elasticity.

The Mind as Creator

Beyond observation and interpretation lies creation. The mind does not merely receive and analyze, it generates. Creativity is not limited to artists or inventors. Every decision, hypothesis, and solution begins as an act of imagination, a leap from what is to what might be.

Creativity flourishes in a relaxed yet attentive mind. Pressure suppresses it, curiosity feeds it. A scientist who daydreams about a problem may stumble upon a breakthrough precisely because the mind, freed from urgency, can roam freely.

In a sense, deep thinking is creative. It rearranges the known to reveal the unknown. The thinker who can imagine alternatives expands the possible. The one who cannot is trapped in habit.

The Emotional Mind

The mind and emotion are not separate rooms, they are adjoining spaces with a shared door. Emotion energizes thought. Without feeling, there is no motivation to inquire or act. Yet emotion, when unchecked, distorts. Fear narrows perspective. Anger magnifies grievance. Joy can lead to rash optimism.

Balanced thought requires emotional literacy, the ability to recognize what you feel, why you feel it, and how it colors your reasoning. The emotionally aware thinker does not suppress feeling, he studies it as data. Emotions are signals, not commands.

Consider a negotiator who senses irritation rising during a tense meeting. Instead of reacting, she notes it, pauses, and redirects her tone. She has not eliminated emotion, she has integrated it into awareness. The result is clarity with humanity, reason guided by compassion.

Memory and Its Shadows

Memory shapes thought by linking past to present. It provides context for decisions, continuity for identity, and evidence for reasoning. But memory is fallible. It edits, compresses, and occasionally invents.

What we recall is often a reconstruction, influenced by current emotion. A happy memory can sour when revisited in bitterness, and a painful one can soften with forgiveness. Memory does not replay events, it rewrites them.

Skilled thinkers treat memory as a useful but unreliable witness. They verify recollection against fact, much as a scientist tests a hypothesis. Doing so prevents the mind from becoming a prisoner of its own stories.

Bias and Distortion

All minds contain bias. It is the residue of experience, culture, and preference. Bias is not always malicious, it helps the brain simplify decisions. But when it is unconscious, it warps reasoning.

Common biases include confirmation bias, which favors evidence that supports what we already believe, anchoring bias, which relies too heavily on first impressions, and availability bias, which judges probability by what easily comes to mind. These shortcuts save time, but they sacrifice truth.

To counter bias, expose the mind to diversity of ideas, people, and experiences. Question certainties. Seek disagreement from intelligent peers. The point is not to destroy conviction, but to refine it through friction.

The Rational Mind

Reasoning distinguishes human thought from instinct. It organizes perception, weighs alternatives, and predicts outcomes. Rationality is not cold logic, it is disciplined curiosity.

Strong reasoning begins with definition. Many arguments are endless because the participants never agreed on what they were discussing. A good thinker clarifies terms before debating them. Then, reasoning proceeds by evidence and inference, not emotion or authority.

Logic is the skeleton of sound thought. Emotion gives it flesh. Together, they form the full anatomy of understanding.

An attorney once described reasoning as "the art of building a staircase between facts and conclusions." Weak thinkers skip steps. Strong ones build every tread.

The Intuitive Mind

Intuition is the mind's subconscious reasoning, a rapid synthesis of experience that is too quick for conscious logic. It often feels like a sudden knowing. Intuition is not magic, it is compressed wisdom.

Experienced professionals rely on intuition when time forbids analysis, a doctor diagnosing by instinct, a pilot reacting to turbulence, a musician adjusting tempo by feel. Their intuition works because it is trained.

To develop intuition, feed it with observation, experience, and feedback. The subconscious mind integrates patterns only when it has patterns to draw from. Intuition without knowledge is guesswork. Intuition informed by mastery is genius.

The Reflective Mind

Reflection is the mind observing itself, the highest form of awareness. It asks, "What am I thinking, and why?" Without reflection, thought becomes automatic. With reflection, thought becomes deliberate.

Reflection transforms experience into understanding. After a conversation, a mistake, or a success, pausing to review what occurred solidifies learning. Journaling, meditation, and solitude cultivate this reflective state.

Self-reflection also reveals contradiction. The thinker who notices gaps between belief and behavior gains honesty. As Socrates observed, "The unexamined life is not worth living." The examined one becomes a map of growth.

The Focused and the Wandering Mind

The mind alternates between two modes, focused and diffuse. The focused mind is analytical, it dissects. The diffuse mind is associative, it connects. Both are vital.

In focus, we compute and conclude. In wandering, we create. Many breakthroughs occur not at the desk but in the shower, in the garden, or during a quiet walk. The thinker who can shift between these modes at will gains command of mental rhythm.

When overfocused, the mind tightens. When too diffuse, it drifts. Balance restores productivity and imagination alike.

Chapter 6: Who Is Responsible for Your Ability to Think?

The ability to think is both a gift and a duty. Every person is born with a mind capable of learning, questioning, and choosing, but not everyone develops that mind to its full potential. The responsibility for doing so does not belong to teachers, governments, or families alone. It belongs first and last to you.

We live in a world that encourages dependence. From childhood, we are told what to believe, what to fear, and what to value. Schools teach facts, employers teach procedures, and media supply opinions ready for repetition. Thinking independently takes effort, and effort is what most people quietly avoid. Yet the health of a mind, like that of a muscle, depends on the work it performs. A neglected mind becomes weak, a disciplined one grows powerful.

The Chain of Responsibility

Responsibility for thought begins early. Parents plant the first seeds by encouraging curiosity, by answering questions instead of silencing them. A child who is told, "Because I said so," learns obedience; a child who is told, "Let's figure it out," learns reasoning. Those two paths diverge early and rarely meet again.

But even the most thoughtful upbringing can only go so far. Eventually, each person must take ownership of their own mental habits. No parent, teacher, or mentor can think for another. They can light the lamp, but you must tend the flame. A student may blame a poor education for ignorance, but self-education remains forever available. The shelves of every library, the pages of history, and now the digital archives of the world sit open to anyone with curiosity and persistence.

Benjamin Franklin, who left school at ten, became one of the most learned people of his time by reading late into the night. Abraham Lincoln taught himself law from borrowed books by candlelight. Neither man waited for permission to learn; they accepted responsibility for their own minds. That decision, the conscious acceptance of mental responsibility, marks the difference between an informed citizen and a compliant follower.

The Habit of Asking "Why?"

Independent thinking begins with a question. The child who asks *why* grows into the adult who asks *how* and *what if*. Every discovery in history began with someone unwilling to accept the first answer given. "Why does the apple fall?" "Why does illness spread?" "Why can't ordinary people rule themselves?" These questions changed science, medicine, and government alike.

But asking *why* can be uncomfortable. It challenges authority, disturbs tradition, and exposes ignorance. That is precisely why it matters. The habit of asking *why* is the antidote to mental laziness. It is how the mind stays alive.

When you encounter an idea, especially one that flatters your existing beliefs, pause and ask:

• Why do I believe this?
• Who benefits if I accept it?
• What evidence supports or contradicts it?

These questions transform passive acceptance into active reasoning. They make you responsible not just for what you think, but for how you think.

The Role of Education and Its Limits

Formal education introduces knowledge, but it does not guarantee thought. Many graduates can recite formulas or quote theories yet cannot explain them in their own words. True education is not memorization; it is mental training, the strengthening of comprehension, analysis, and judgment.

Socrates taught not by lecturing but by questioning. His students learned to discover truth through dialogue, to expose contradictions in their own reasoning. That method remains the foundation of genuine education. Unfortunately, modern schooling often rewards conformity more than curiosity. Students learn to supply the expected answer rather than explore possibilities. The result is a culture of intellectual dependency, people who wait for someone else to tell them what is true.

The responsibility for correcting that pattern lies with each learner. Read beyond the assigned material. Test information against real-world results. When a teacher, pundit, or politician makes a claim, verify it yourself. In the digital age, ignorance is not the absence of information, it is the refusal to examine it.

The Influence of Culture and Media

Culture shapes how we think, often more than we realize. Every society carries invisible assumptions about success, morality, gender, and authority. Media amplify these assumptions, reinforcing them until they appear natural.

Advertisements tell us what to desire; social networks tell us what to fear. Algorithms feed us what we already agree with, turning the mind into an echo chamber.

To remain a free thinker within such a system requires vigilance. Ask yourself daily, whose thoughts am I repeating? If a phrase or opinion comes too easily to mind, something heard in headlines or slogans, pause before adopting it. The speed of information has outpaced our ability to digest it, therefore we must slow down deliberately. Reflection is the new rebellion.

The responsibility of the modern thinker is to separate fact from persuasion. Every image, every "viral" story carries a motive. The thoughtful person asks what that motive is before reacting emotionally. The reward for this effort is clarity, the rarest currency in an age of noise.

Emotional Responsibility

Thinking is not purely intellectual; it is emotional discipline as well. Feelings shape our reasoning more than we care to admit. Anger narrows focus, fear exaggerates risk, desire distorts value. The responsible thinker does not suppress emotion but learns to recognize and balance it.

Consider a juror in a courtroom. Sympathy for the victim must not override fairness to the accused. Logic must temper compassion. Likewise, in daily life, emotion can inform thought without commanding it. You cannot think clearly about what you desperately want or dread until you step back enough to see the situation whole. Emotional responsibility means noticing when the heart begins steering the mind and gently taking back the wheel.

One practical method is the emotional audit. When faced with a decision, list the feelings present, anger, pride, guilt, hope, and ask how each one might bias your judgment. Awareness alone often restores balance.

The Mind as Steward

Every mind influences others. Parents model thinking for children; leaders model it for followers; writers and teachers model it for readers and students. Whether you intend it or not, your thinking teaches. Each careless opinion you repeat, each unexamined prejudice you pass along, shapes the thinking of those who hear you. To think responsibly is therefore an ethical act.

History shows how easily masses can be led when they surrender personal judgment. Propaganda succeeds not because lies are powerful, but because people stop questioning them. The German philosopher Hannah Arendt observed that the first step toward tyranny is not cruelty but thoughtlessness, a refusal to examine the meaning of one's own actions. The antidote is individual reflection, multiplied by millions.

When you hold yourself responsible for your own thoughts, you also become responsible for their ripple effect. A calm, rational voice in a fearful crowd can restore reason to many. Conversely, one reckless statement from an admired figure can ignite chaos. The mature thinker understands this and treats words as instruments, not weapons.

Overcoming the Temptation to Conform

Human beings crave belonging. It is easier to agree than to stand alone. But conformity is the silent killer of thought. When people value acceptance more than accuracy, truth withers. The responsible thinker must occasionally risk disapproval.

History honors those who did. Galileo questioned Church doctrine and redefined the universe. Rosa Parks refused to surrender her seat and reignited a movement. Neither sought fame; both acted from conviction rooted in thought. Each asked a simple question, "Is this right?" and accepted responsibility for the answer.

You need not face persecution to practice that courage. It might mean disagreeing politely in conversation, voting according to conscience rather than tribe, or admitting uncertainty when others pretend to know. Independent thought requires moral backbone, the willingness to be wrong in public until proven right.

The Role of Habit and Environment

Responsibility for thinking also includes the environments we choose. The company we keep influences what ideas seem normal. Spend time among cynics, and optimism begins to feel naïve. Spend time among creators, and possibility becomes contagious.

Protect your mental diet as carefully as your physical one. Limit exposure to those who thrive on outrage or triviality. Seek those who challenge you respectfully, who make you think harder, not angrier. A conversation with one honest critic can refine your ideas more than a hundred affirmations from admirers.

Habits matter as well. Set aside time daily for undistracted thought, ten minutes of solitude can reset the mind more effectively than an hour of noise. Keep a notebook of questions rather than answers. The act of writing thoughts down, however roughly, transforms vague impressions into clarity. The responsible thinker treats thinking itself as a daily practice, not an occasional exercise.

Accountability for Mental Growth

Responsibility for thought includes responsibility for growth. To stop learning is to stop living. The world changes, so must the mind. New knowledge demands revision of old beliefs. Pride resists this, but humility embraces it.

Ask yourself regularly, when was the last time I changed my mind for a good reason? If the answer is "I can't remember," stagnation has begun. Growth means welcoming correction without shame. It also means admitting when experience has disproved theory. Wisdom is not consistency; it is alignment with truth as it unfolds.

Lifelong learners, scientists, artists, entrepreneurs, understand this instinctively. They treat curiosity as maintenance, not luxury. They are responsible for keeping their minds current, flexible, and ready to adapt. You can do the same, regardless of age or profession. The brain rewires itself continuously; the only requirement is willingness.

The Moral Dimension of Thinking

Thinking is not morally neutral. How you use your mind affects others. A clever lie, a manipulative argument, a calculated omission, each misuses the gift of thought. Responsibility for thinking therefore includes integrity.

Intelligence without morality becomes exploitation. History's most notorious figures were often brilliant strategists who used reason for cruelty. Wisdom requires conscience. Every time you form an opinion, ask not only "Is this true?" but "Is this good?" Ethics is reasoning applied to the welfare of others.

This moral responsibility extends to collective thought as well. Democracies depend on citizens who reason before reacting, who verify before voting, who question before condemning. The health of a nation mirrors the integrity of its thinking citizens. To think irresponsibly, to spread rumors, to share anger disguised as fact, is to corrode that foundation. Each mind that insists on honesty strengthens the whole.

Thinking as Self-Governance

The philosopher Ernest Dimnet, whose ideas inspired this book, argued that the greatest freedom is freedom of mind. He warned that most people live as mental dependents, ruled by external authority rather than inner judgment. To reclaim that authority is an act of self-governance.

Your mind is your government. Its laws are your values, its currency is attention, its citizens are your thoughts. Rule it wisely. Let reason debate emotion, let experience inform imagination, let conscience oversee ambition. When these forces balance, the mind becomes a stable democracy rather than a dictatorship of impulse.

Freedom of thought carries the same burden as political freedom, responsibility. You must defend it daily against invasion, by distraction, propaganda, or despair. The greatest tyrant you will ever face is your own apathy. Guard your independence fiercely, and your mind will remain your own.

Teaching Responsibility By Example

Responsibility for thinking can be taught, but only by demonstration. Children, students, employees, and friends learn not from lectures but from behavior. When you admit error publicly, you teach humility. When you research before speaking, you teach diligence. When you change your view after hearing evidence, you teach courage.

Every environment, home, school, workplace, community, needs examples of thoughtful conduct. These examples ripple outward invisibly. A parent who reasons calmly with a child plants seeds of reason for the next generation. A manager who listens before judging trains others to do the same. The culture of thought spreads the way light does, from one flame to another.

The Reward of Ownership

Taking full responsibility for your thinking may seem burdensome at first. It means no more excuses, no more blaming ignorance on teachers or bias on society. But it also brings liberation. When you own your mind, you reclaim control of your life. No insult can define you, no manipulation can mislead you for long, and no failure can destroy you without your consent.

The mind you build becomes your companion, guide, and defense. It interprets the world through clarity instead of confusion. It becomes the difference between drifting through circumstances and directing them.

Responsibility for thinking begins with awareness, grows through practice, and matures into integrity. It is the foundation of freedom and the measure of character. Others may influence what you know, but only you decide how deeply you understand it, how honestly you use it, and how courageously you live by it.

Your ability to think is the most personal possession you will ever have. Guard it. Strengthen it. Use it with care and conviction. For as long as you think for yourself, no one else can ever truly own you.

The Moral Dimension of Thought

Thought is not neutral. Every decision carries consequences for others. The mind's ethical dimension separates wisdom from cleverness. Intelligence can manipulate, wisdom restrains. To think well includes considering the effects of our thinking.

The moral mind measures outcomes not just by success, but by integrity. When honesty and empathy guide thought, decisions gain durability. History remembers not only what people achieved, but how they achieved it.

The Mind in Dialogue

The mind grows sharper through exchange. Discussion exposes blind spots, challenges assumptions, and refines expression. The solitary thinker may reach depth, but conversation widens the field.

Socrates taught through questioning, and the method endures because it reveals what people genuinely think. Dialogue, when conducted respectfully, is the polishing wheel of intellect.

To converse well, listen as intently as you speak. The goal is not victory, the goal is discovery. The best conversations leave both minds enlarged.

Cultivating Awareness

Awareness is the thread that ties all characteristics of mind together. The aware thinker notices thought as it forms, including its motives, tone, and drift. This metacognition allows self-correction in real time.

When awareness fades, thought runs on autopilot, repeating habits and fears. When awareness is active, thought becomes skillful and responsive. Awareness is the gatekeeper of mental freedom.

Like physical fitness, awareness strengthens through daily use, including pausing before reacting, labeling thoughts without judgment, and examining motives before action.

The mind, in all its layers, rational, emotional, intuitive, and moral, is both the instrument and the subject of our greatest work. Understanding its characteristics allows us to use it rather than be used by it. In the next chapter, we will turn to the obstacles that interfere with thought, the inner and outer barriers that confuse, mislead, and sometimes defeat even the best of minds.

Chapter 7: Who Thinks; Who Does Not

Not everyone who appears thoughtful is genuinely thinking. Many people go through life reacting rather than reasoning, repeating rather than questioning. They speak the words of others, defend opinions they never formed, and follow paths they never chose. To think is to live deliberately. To avoid thinking is to drift. The world is divided less by wealth, race, or power than by this single difference, those who think, and those who do not.

The Nature of a Thinking Person

A thinking person is curious, observant, and reflective. They notice what others ignore. They pause before speaking and question before agreeing. They may appear slow to decide, but their decisions hold weight because they have examined both cause and consequence.

The thinking person learns from error. Instead of defending mistakes, they analyze them. They ask, "What went wrong? What did I miss? What can I learn?" Each failure becomes a classroom. This habit separates thinkers from reactors. The non-thinker feels embarrassment and stops. The thinker feels curiosity and grows.

Thinking people are not necessarily scholars or intellectuals. They exist in every profession and class. A mechanic who notices patterns of wear in engines, a nurse who connects symptoms others overlook, a carpenter who senses when a wall is out of plumb without measuring, all are thinkers in their craft. Thinking is not education, it is attention guided by reason.

A thinker also listens differently. They do not wait for their turn to speak. They absorb, analyze, and compare what they hear to what they already know. They are willing to say, "I don't know," because they value truth more than pride. This humility, paradoxically, is the root of their strength.

The Non-Thinker

The non-thinker is not stupid. They may have intelligence, but they do not use it deliberately. They let impulse, habit, or authority make their choices. Their minds function automatically, running on beliefs absorbed from family, media, or social groups. They are mentally alive but unself-aware, like a computer executing someone else's code.

The non-thinker speaks often and listens rarely. They prefer certainty to truth, comfort to clarity. When confronted with a new idea, they do not test it, they reject it. Their opinions are armor, not instruments. To change them would threaten identity, so they defend them fiercely even when evidence crumbles.

The tragedy is that non-thinkers often seem confident. They speak loudly, certain of what they believe. But confidence without examination is only noise. Their energy misleads the timid into silence, giving illusion of majority where only volume exists.

How People Stop Thinking

No one is born a non-thinker. Children question everything. They touch, taste, and ask endlessly. Then, slowly, the world teaches them to stop. Parents tired of questions answer with "Because I said so." Schools reward memorization. Social groups mock difference. Over time, curiosity fades and compliance replaces it.

The process is quiet but devastating. A young mind learns that asking "why" risks embarrassment. It learns that standing alone brings ridicule. It learns that blending in feels safer than being right. So it stops thinking deeply. It repeats. It conforms. It survives but does not grow.

Adults often reinforce this pattern without realizing it. They consume entertainment that tells them what to feel, news that confirms what they already believe, and routines that numb reflection. The mind becomes busy but not active, informed but not enlightened.

Why People Avoid Thinking

Thinking requires effort. It exposes contradiction and demands honesty. Many prefer distraction to discovery because discovery may require change. It is easier to blame luck, politics, or fate than to examine personal responsibility.

Fear also plays a role. To think is to see clearly, and clarity can be painful. It reveals mistakes, illusions, and hypocrisies. Many would rather remain comfortably misled than face uncomfortable truth. As philosopher Søren Kierkegaard observed, "People demand freedom of speech as a compensation for the freedom of thought which they seldom use."

Pride is another obstacle. Admitting error wounds ego. Yet growth begins only where ego ends. The thinker must accept being wrong today to be wiser tomorrow. The non-thinker clings to the illusion of being right even when experience proves otherwise.

The Illusion of Thinking

Some people believe they are thinking when they are only rearranging prejudice. They collect facts that support their views, then call it reasoning. They quote authorities but never verify. They debate not to understand but to win. This is pseudo-thinking, a counterfeit form of reason that flatters ignorance with sophistication.

Social media amplifies this illusion. People skim headlines and form instant opinions. They confuse reaction with reflection, emotion with evidence. Clicking "like" replaces learning. The appearance of engagement hides the absence of comprehension. The mind becomes a mirror reflecting what it already believes.

True thinking requires time and solitude. It begins when distraction ends. It grows in silence, where the mind can listen to itself without noise. A person who never spends time alone with their thoughts may live surrounded by information yet starved of insight.

The Courage to Think

Thinking takes courage because it separates you from the crowd. The moment you question what others accept, you risk being labeled difficult or disloyal. History punishes thinkers first, then honors them later. Socrates was executed for corrupting youth, Galileo was condemned for observing truth, reformers of every age faced ridicule before recognition.

To think independently in your own time is to endure isolation. Yet that isolation is the forge of wisdom. The mind that cannot stand alone will never stand at all. Independence of thought begins when you stop fearing disapproval.

Courageous thinkers are not reckless. They test their conclusions carefully. They know that defiance without evidence is as foolish as obedience without question. Their strength lies in balance, the ability to disagree without hostility and to persist without arrogance.

Thinking and Self-Awareness

Thinking begins with awareness of self. To know your biases, habits, and emotions is to understand how they shape your reasoning. Many people skip this step. They assume they are objective when in truth they are guided by hidden motives.

Metacognition, the ability to watch your own thoughts, is the hallmark of a developed mind. It allows you to notice when emotion takes over, when attention drifts, or when assumptions replace evidence. Without self-awareness, intellect becomes a tool of justification rather than discovery.

A self-aware thinker can admit contradiction and adjust course. They do not mistake stubbornness for strength. They know that truth is not loyalty to an old belief, but accuracy in the present one.

The Social Consequences of Not Thinking

When individuals stop thinking, societies decay. History repeats its worst chapters whenever people trade judgment for slogans. Totalitarian regimes depend on unthinking obedience. Economic bubbles grow when investors follow crowds instead of analysis. Wars erupt when nations mistake emotion for logic.

Propaganda succeeds only where reflection fails. A population trained to question cannot be easily deceived. A population trained to obey will accept any narrative, however absurd, if it comes from authority. The cost of collective unthinking is measured in wasted lives and lost freedom.

Every democracy depends on thinkers, citizens who verify facts, interpret laws, and hold power accountable. When they grow passive, leaders grow corrupt. When they grow fearful, demagogues rise. Thought is not only personal virtue but civic defense.

Thinking and Work

In the workplace, the difference between thinkers and non-thinkers is visible in outcomes. The non-thinker performs tasks as given. The thinker improves them. The non-thinker waits for orders. The thinker anticipates needs. Employers may value obedience, but organizations thrive only through thoughtful initiative.

In creative fields, thinking turns repetition into innovation. A chef who questions a recipe discovers a new flavor. An engineer who studies failures designs safer machines. A leader who listens to subordinates prevents crises. Thinking multiplies skill. It is the unseen ingredient behind every sustainable success.

Yet many workplaces discourage thought by rewarding compliance. Meetings become rituals of agreement. Questioning is seen as challenge. When fear of error exceeds curiosity for improvement, progress halts. The responsible worker must learn to think even within systems that prefer silence.

The Role of Technology

Technology has made information abundant but understanding scarce. The more data we have, the less we digest. Devices supply answers before we form questions. Search engines complete our sentences. Algorithms predict our interests. Convenience replaces contemplation.

There is nothing wrong with technology itself. The danger lies in dependence. When machines do our remembering, pattern-finding, and decision-making, mental muscle weakens. We risk becoming users of tools we no longer understand.

The responsible thinker uses technology as a servant, not a master. They verify sources, question motives, and seek context. They treat information as raw material, not final truth. In an age of automation, the most human act is still to think.

Signs of a Thinking Mind

You can recognize a thinker not by education or profession, but by habit. They read widely, listen carefully, and speak thoughtfully. They avoid gossip, exaggeration, and empty argument. They enjoy discussion more than victory. They correct themselves easily. They ask questions that make others pause.

A thinking person values silence as much as conversation. They are comfortable being alone because solitude sharpens reflection. They are patient with complexity but intolerant of deceit. They prefer to understand rather than to judge. And they know that thinking, like health, must be maintained daily or it declines.

Signs of an Unthinking Mind

The unthinking person avoids silence. They fill it with noise, chatter, or screens. They mistake activity for accomplishment. They are restless in reflection and uncomfortable with uncertainty. They rely on emotion to decide and on authority to justify. Their opinions change with their company.

Unthinking people are easy to lead and easy to deceive. They believe what feels right, not what is true. Their confidence comes from numbers, not from knowledge. When surrounded by others who think the same way, they feel safe, but that safety is illusion. Herds move together not because each member is wise, but because none can bear to be left behind.

The Discipline of Independent Thought

To move from non-thinking to thinking requires discipline. Start by setting aside time each day for reflection. Read something that disagrees with you. Summarize complex ideas in your own words. Ask why you believe what you do. Write it down. The act of writing forces precision. Precision reveals gaps. Gaps invite learning.

Engage in calm debate. Not every disagreement is conflict. Seek discussion with those who think differently but honestly.

Avoid those who argue to win rather than to understand. Truth emerges through collaboration, not conquest.

Practice observation. Notice small details in daily life, the tone of a voice, the design of a system, the reaction of others. Thinking begins in noticing. Most people look but do not see. The world is full of lessons invisible to those who rush.

Finally, embrace boredom. In quiet moments, when nothing demands your attention, the mind begins to create. Modern life fears stillness, but stillness is where thought matures. The greatest ideas in history were born in silence, not noise.

The Thinker's Reward

Thinking does not guarantee happiness, but it guarantees meaning. When you think, you understand yourself and your world. You see connections others miss. You suffer fewer regrets because your choices are conscious. You act with purpose instead of impulse. The reward is not fame or wealth but self-respect.

Thinking also brings peace. The mind trained to examine itself does not fear contradiction. It knows that confusion precedes clarity. It accepts uncertainty as part of growth. The unthinking mind feels chaos as threat, the thinking mind sees it as raw material for wisdom.

A thinker may feel alone at times, but never empty. Their own mind becomes companion and teacher. They live with awareness rather than habit. They may age, but they never grow old in spirit.

The difference between thinkers and non-thinkers defines the quality of every life and every society. Those who think lead, innovate, and elevate. Those who do not drift, follow, and repeat. The world will always have both, but the future belongs to those who choose thought over reaction, reason over noise, and truth over comfort.

Thinking is not a privilege, it is a responsibility. It is the act that keeps civilization alive. If you wish to rise above confusion, cultivate your mind daily. Learn, question, reflect, and decide. Be one of the few who genuinely think, for through your example, others may remember how.

Chapter 8: Distractions

Distraction is the enemy of thought. It breaks focus, scatters purpose, and dulls awareness. Modern life trains us not to think deeply but to react instantly. We check, scroll, click, and reply without pause. What once demanded minutes of reflection now vanishes in seconds of attention. The world around us runs on noise, and those who control the noise control the minds of the distracted.

The Nature of Distraction

Distraction is not only the loss of attention; it is the theft of intention. It draws the mind away from what matters toward what shouts loudest. In the past, distraction came from external interruptions , a ringing phone, a knock at the door, a sudden noise. Today, distraction lives inside our own hands. We carry it with us. Our devices interrupt even silence, flooding it with alerts and updates that seem important but rarely are.

The distracted mind becomes restless even in calm surroundings. It cannot sit still or think long. It seeks stimulation the way a thirsty person seeks water, yet the more it drinks, the drier it feels. This is because stimulation is not satisfaction. The mind craves meaning, not motion.

How Distraction Works

Distraction hijacks the brain's reward system. Each notification, each new piece of information, gives a small burst of pleasure. It feels like progress but produces nothing. This reward loop trains the mind to prefer novelty over depth. The result is a population that knows many things slightly but few things well.

Marketers understand this perfectly. The attention economy turns distraction into profit. Every app, every feed, every news site competes for seconds of your awareness. They design colors, sounds, and motion to keep you hooked. Their success depends on your failure to focus.

Distraction also exploits emotion. Anger, outrage, and fear hold attention longer than calm thought. That is why so much of modern media is built on conflict. It keeps people engaged, not enlightened. You scroll through outrage, share it, react to it, and in the end, nothing changes except your peace of mind.

The Cost of Distraction

The price of distraction is measured in lost potential. Ideas that could have grown into action die halfway formed. Goals are delayed until urgency fades. Relationships suffer when presence is replaced by partial attention. Distraction steals the minutes that form meaning.

At work, distraction destroys efficiency. A single interruption can take minutes to recover from, yet people accept constant interruption as normal. They switch between emails, calls, and messages so often that deep work becomes impossible. They end the day exhausted but unfulfilled, having done much but achieved little.

In personal life, distraction erodes intimacy. Families sit together but communicate through screens. Conversations shrink into fragments. Memory weakens because nothing is fully experienced. The distracted person lives in a blur of motion without reflection, activity without awareness.

The Illusion of Multitasking

Many believe they can handle distraction through multitasking. They think they can divide attention without losing quality. Science proves otherwise. The brain cannot fully focus on two complex tasks at once. It merely switches rapidly, losing time and accuracy with each change. What feels efficient is actually wasteful.

Multitasking turns the mind into a juggler, always moving, never mastering. It fragments thought and weakens memory. The thinker who tries to do everything ends up doing nothing well. Concentration is not a limitation; it is power. A single focused hour produces more value than a distracted day.

The Distraction of Busyness

Some distractions disguise themselves as productivity. People fill calendars, answer emails, attend meetings, and feel important. Yet much of that activity is avoidance in disguise. It protects them from confronting harder questions , what matters, what they genuinely want, what they should stop doing.

Busyness is the most respectable form of distraction. It earns praise while wasting life. The busy person may appear dedicated, but often they are simply afraid to slow down. Stillness would expose emptiness. So they run from silence, mistaking motion for meaning.

Technology Distraction

Technology magnifies distraction by removing natural boundaries. In earlier times, work ended when you left the office. Today, the office follows you home. Notifications bridge every hour. The day has no edges. The mind never fully rests or resets.

Devices also replace human presence with simulated attention. We text instead of talk, react instead of respond. Even entertainment demands divided focus, with one eye on the screen and one on the feed. The result is chronic partial engagement , a mind never fully here or anywhere.

Technology itself is not evil, but it rewards weakness. It offers comfort over control. To master it, one must reclaim choice. Use the tool, do not become it. Turn off alerts. Schedule silence. Treat attention as property, not a public resource.

Mental Clutter

Not all distractions come from outside. Many come from within. Worry, regret, and anticipation crowd the mind as effectively as any device. A person can be alone in a quiet room and still not be free of noise. Internal chatter, self-criticism, and constant planning fragment focus as completely as a hundred notifications.

Clarity begins with mental decluttering. Write down what worries you. Decide which thoughts require action and which deserve release. A problem written is half solved. The rest fades naturally when the mind is no longer trying to juggle it in silence.

Distraction and Emotion

Emotions are powerful drivers of distraction. Anger rushes in to claim attention, fear repeats its warnings, and pleasure tempts repetition. When emotion dominates, reason disappears. Learning to observe emotion without surrendering to it is the discipline that protects thought.

The thinker does not suppress feeling, they notice it. They say, "I am angry," or "I am afraid," without acting on impulse. This simple recognition separates awareness from reaction. The emotion loses control the moment it is named.

Distraction as Escape

For many, distraction is comfort. It shields them from confronting emptiness, grief, or dissatisfaction. Entertainment becomes anesthesia. Social media becomes validation. News becomes outrage therapy. Each offers relief from reflection.

But the more one escapes, the weaker the will becomes. Problems avoided multiply. Meaning fades. The person who always distracts themselves never learns who they are. Silence, though uncomfortable, is necessary for self-understanding.

The Discipline of Focus

Focus is not the absence of distraction, it is the act of returning. Even the strongest mind wanders. The skill is not perfect concentration but persistent correction. Every time you notice your attention drift and bring it back, you strengthen control.

To rebuild focus, begin small. Practice doing one task with full attention , reading a page, listening to a song, completing a chore. Gradually lengthen the time before interruption. Over days and weeks, your ability to hold thought increases.

Rituals help. Work in the same space each day. Clear your desk. Silence notifications. Take short breaks but avoid constant checking. Train your environment to support attention rather than divide it.

The Value of Boredom

Boredom is misunderstood. It is not a problem; it is a signal. It tells you the mind is underused. When you allow boredom, the brain begins to create. Daydreaming connects scattered ideas. Insight often arrives when stimulation ends.

Children once developed imagination through boredom. Now every quiet moment is filled with screens. As a result, creativity declines. To think deeply, you must reclaim boredom as practice. Let the mind wander without input. Allow silence to stretch until curiosity returns on its own.

Social Distraction

Society rewards noise. Those who shout loudest gather followers. Constant connection is treated as virtue, while solitude is mistaken for loneliness. Yet thinkers throughout history have sought solitude not to escape others but to see them more clearly.

Social distraction can also take subtler forms , endless discussion, gossip, and approval seeking. The desire to be liked can drown the desire to be right. The thinker must sometimes disappoint others to remain honest with themselves.

The Politics of Distraction

Governments and institutions understand that distraction weakens resistance. When citizens are entertained, divided, or angry at each other, they pay less attention to what truly matters. Bread and circuses remain the oldest political tools.

The responsible citizen must therefore protect focus as a civic duty. Read original sources. Verify claims. Pay attention to what is not being said. Awareness is power; distraction is surrender. The health of democracy depends on attentive minds more than on passionate hearts.

The Economics of Attention

In today's economy, attention is currency. Companies buy it, sell it, and harvest it through algorithms. The more distracted you are, the richer someone else becomes. Every click, scroll, or view generates value for others while costing you time.

To reclaim independence, treat your attention like money. Spend it wisely. Invest it in learning, creating, or connecting. Avoid paying it to those who only profit from your distraction. Attention, once lost, cannot be earned back.

Reclaiming Control

To overcome distraction, start by observing it. Keep a small record of when your focus breaks and why. Notice patterns , certain times, places, or emotions. Awareness turns unconscious habit into conscious choice.

Then simplify. Remove unneeded apps, silence alerts, set limits. Design your day around priorities, not interruptions.

95

Begin each morning with intention rather than reaction. A few quiet minutes spent planning save hours later.

Protect time for reflection. Read without screens nearby. Walk without music. Eat without your phone. Let moments breathe. The world will not fall apart if you disconnect for a while, but your mind may heal in the space left open.

The Reward of Attention

Attention is life's most valuable currency. What you attend to shapes who you become. When you focus on fear, you grow anxious. When you focus on gratitude, you grow peaceful. When you focus on problems, they multiply. When you focus on purpose, they diminish.

Attention determines experience. A distracted mind sees fragments; a focused mind sees patterns. Thought requires sustained attention the way fire requires oxygen. Remove it and understanding dies.

The thinker therefore guards attention as sacred. They do not let noise dictate direction. They choose what to see, what to hear, and what to ignore. In doing so, they gain something rare in modern life , clarity.

Distraction weakens the mind, shortens memory, and steals time. It promises pleasure but delivers emptiness. Those who master attention reclaim their lives from chaos. The power to think deeply, to act decisively, and to live meaningfully depends on one skill , the ability to stay present.

Guard your attention as you would your freedom. Both can be lost without notice. Choose focus over frenzy, silence over noise, substance over spectacle. The world will not help you do this, but your own mind will thank you.

Chapter 9: Concentration

Concentration is the muscle of thought. Without it, the mind drifts. Ideas blur. Tasks begin but never finish. Success in anything worthwhile depends on the ability to hold attention on one thing long enough for it to mature. Concentration is not luck or talent. It is training.

Every great work of art, invention, or discovery began with focus sustained over time. Edison, Beethoven, and Einstein each had extraordinary powers of attention. They did not simply work harder; they worked longer on one line of thought while others became distracted. Concentration is the bridge between curiosity and mastery.

The Meaning of Concentration

To concentrate is to gather the mind's scattered energy into a single stream. The average person's attention jumps constantly, pulled by sound, movement, and emotion. A concentrated mind is different. It does not chase every passing thought. It selects one and stays with it. Concentration is deliberate control of mental energy.

Concentration also means awareness without strain. It is not tightening the mind but steadying it. Think of it as holding a glass of water perfectly level rather than gripping it tightly. True concentration feels calm and powerful, not forced. It is the art of staying with what is in front of you until understanding appears.

Why Concentration Matters

In an age of endless distraction, concentration has become rare. People pride themselves on multitasking, yet they accomplish less. Each interruption breaks mental rhythm. Studies show that after a distraction, it can take several minutes to recover full focus. Multiply that by dozens of interruptions a day, and you lose hours.

Concentration creates quality. A writer who gives full attention to one sentence writes truthfully. A surgeon who focuses entirely on one incision saves lives. A leader who listens without distraction earns trust. The power to concentrate determines not only productivity but also integrity. It reveals what we value enough to give our full mind.

The Science of Concentration

Modern research confirms what ancient thinkers knew: the human brain cannot sustain deep focus indefinitely, but it can train itself to return quickly after wandering. Concentration depends on two systems working together , attention and inhibition. One brings focus to the chosen task, the other suppresses distractions.

Neuroscientists describe this balance as top-down control. The prefrontal cortex, the brain's executive center, tells other regions what to ignore. The more you practice this control, the stronger it becomes. Like a muscle, attention grows through repetition and rest. You cannot force it endlessly, but you can strengthen it steadily.

The Flow State

At its highest level, concentration becomes flow , a state of full immersion where time disappears. In flow, effort feels effortless. The painter forgets the brush, the athlete forgets the body, and the thinker forgets the clock. Flow combines focus, challenge, and enjoyment. It is the purest form of concentration because it unites action and awareness.

To enter flow, three conditions help: clear goals, immediate feedback, and a task that is difficult but possible. Too easy and the mind grows bored. Too hard and it grows anxious. The sweet spot of challenge keeps attention alive. This is why skilled work can be deeply satisfying. It holds the mind completely.

Training Concentration

Concentration grows by practice, not promise. It begins with short periods of focused effort, repeated daily. Start with a single task , reading, writing, or studying , and commit to it for a set time without switching. Even ten minutes of uninterrupted focus strengthens the mind. Gradually lengthen the time as endurance improves.

The Pomodoro Technique offers one simple method. Work for twenty-five minutes, then rest for five. After four rounds, take a longer break. This rhythm mirrors the brain's natural cycles of alertness. The key is not the timer but the rule: during focus time, do nothing else. No phone, no checking, no side task.

Another method is to create rituals of beginning. Sit in the same place, arrange the same tools, or perform a small routine before each period of work. The mind learns to associate those cues with focus. Like an athlete stretching before a race, ritual prepares attention for effort.

Environment and Concentration

The environment shapes the mind more than most realize. Noise, clutter, and interruptions drain mental energy even when you try to ignore them. A quiet, orderly space signals the brain that focus is safe. It reduces the need for vigilance and frees energy for thought.

Choose a workspace that feels calm. Remove unnecessary objects from sight. Keep your tools within reach. Limit background sounds. If noise cannot be avoided, use low instrumental music or white noise to create a steady atmosphere. The goal is not silence, but stability.

Lighting also matters. Natural light keeps energy steady, while harsh or dim light fatigues the eyes. Temperature affects alertness. Small discomforts accumulate and weaken concentration, so control what you can. Every environmental improvement strengthens attention indirectly.

The Role of Motivation

No one concentrates well on what they do not care about. Interest fuels focus. When you believe a task matters, attention flows naturally. Motivation turns discipline into enjoyment.

Find a clear purpose behind your work. Ask yourself why it matters, what it leads to, and how it fits your values. Purpose converts duty into devotion. The writer who sees meaning in their message stays at the desk when others quit. The student who connects study to future growth reads with energy instead of fatigue.

If motivation fades, break goals into smaller steps. Each small completion restores momentum. Concentration often collapses not from difficulty but from vagueness. You cannot focus on what you cannot define.

The Enemy of Concentration: Restlessness

Restlessness is the internal form of distraction. It appears as impatience, boredom, or anxiety. The restless mind fears stillness. It jumps from one thing to another, mistaking movement for progress. Yet progress begins when the mind stops running away from discomfort.

The cure for restlessness is presence. When your attention wanders, gently bring it back. Do not scold yourself. Concentration improves through repetition, not punishment. Every time you notice distraction and return, you build strength.

Breathing exercises can help calm mental restlessness. Slow, deep breaths reduce tension and stabilize attention. Even one minute of steady breathing can reset the mind between tasks. Physical calm supports mental clarity.

Concentration and Time

Time is the partner of concentration. Focus determines the value of time, and time tests the endurance of focus. The most successful people are not those who work longest, but those who work most attentively. An hour of full concentration can achieve what a distracted person does in four.

Plan your day around your highest-focus hours. For most people, that is the morning before fatigue accumulates. Protect that time. Schedule demanding tasks then, and reserve easier work for later. Concentration is a limited resource; use it where it counts.

Avoid filling every minute. Breaks renew focus. Short pauses after each period of work prevent burnout. Step away from the task, move, stretch, or take a brief walk. The mind resets through rhythm , focus, release, return.

The Role of Rest

Concentration depends on rest as much as effort. A tired brain cannot focus clearly. Sleep restores the chemical balance required for sustained attention. Skipping rest weakens not only energy but judgment.

Quality rest also means mental distance. Shifting to a different activity, such as walking, cooking, or listening to music, allows subconscious processing. Many insights arrive when you are no longer trying. The mind continues working quietly beneath awareness.

The Illusion of Control

Many lose concentration because they try to control too much. They attempt to manage every detail instead of trusting the process. Concentration requires letting go of what is outside your influence. Control the input , your effort, your attitude, your preparation , and accept that outcomes will come naturally.

An overcontrolled mind becomes tense, and tension breaks focus. Relaxed effort is more powerful than rigid effort. Learn to flow with tasks rather than fight them. Control is not concentration; presence is.

Concentration and Emotion

Emotion can either sharpen or scatter attention. Passion focuses. Anger or fear disperses. When you care deeply about a goal, energy aligns. When you react emotionally, attention fragments.

The skill is emotional regulation. Notice feelings as they arise. Use them to drive effort but not to dominate it. The thinker must feel fully but remain balanced. Concentration requires both heart and discipline.

Techniques for Deep Work

Deep work means working in a state of sustained concentration without distraction. It is rare but powerful. To achieve it, remove all shallow tasks during deep work hours. No browsing, no chatting, no small decisions. Prepare everything in advance so you can stay immersed.

Begin each deep work session with a clear target , a page written, a chapter reviewed, a problem solved. Keep track of progress visibly, such as with a checklist or journal. Completion reinforces motivation and keeps momentum alive.

End sessions intentionally. Write a short summary or reflection before stopping. This closure signals the brain to store what it learned. The next session begins faster because the mind remembers where it left off.

Common Detractors from Concentration

Several habits quietly weaken focus:

1. Constant checking of messages or updates. Each break resets attention.
2. Cluttered workspaces. Visual noise competes for awareness.
3. Poor diet or dehydration. The brain needs steady energy.
4. Lack of sleep. Fatigue shortens attention span.
5. Overcommitment. Too many priorities fragment energy.
6. Negative self-talk. Doubt distracts as much as noise.

Each of these can be improved with intention. Small changes in routine have large effects on attention.

The Habit of Concentration

Concentration is not a momentary act but a habit of mind. It grows through consistency. Choose one activity each day that requires total attention , even washing dishes or driving , and treat it as training. Notice how often the mind wanders and gently returns.

Over time, this practice strengthens awareness in every part of life. You begin to listen better, think deeper, and act with greater precision. Concentration becomes natural rather than forced.

Concentration and Meaning

At its deepest level, concentration connects to meaning. To concentrate is to care. You give something the honor of your full mind. Whatever receives full attention becomes important, and importance gives life structure. Without concentration, everything feels shallow because nothing receives depth.

Meaning grows where attention stays. A person who cannot concentrate cannot fully love, learn, or create. Concentration gives continuity to character. It is the root of excellence, integrity, and peace.

Concentration is the art of staying present with purpose. It requires calm, patience, and repetition. It turns fleeting thoughts into understanding and scattered actions into achievement. Every act of focus builds strength for the next.

To master concentration is to master yourself. Guard your attention as your most valuable possession. Direct it with care, rest it with intention, and use it to shape the life you genuinely want.

Chapter 10: Non-Thinkers and Their Lives

The world is full of people who do not think. They speak, act, and react, but they do not think. Their minds are busy yet shallow, full of motion but empty of meaning. They live by habit, echoing the words and beliefs of others, mistaking repetition for understanding. A life without thought is a life half-lived.

The Non-Thinker's World

To the non-thinker, the world appears simple. There are winners and losers, friends and enemies, good and bad. Every question has an answer already chosen for them by someone else. This simplicity feels safe. It relieves them of the burden of decision. Thinking introduces doubt, and doubt feels like danger.

The non-thinker survives by imitation. They look around, see what others do, and follow. They believe what they are told, especially by those who speak with confidence. Authority replaces analysis. Tradition replaces evidence. Noise replaces truth.

Their conversations are full but not deep. They repeat slogans instead of ideas, opinions instead of insights. They seek agreement, not understanding. To disagree with them is to threaten their comfort, and comfort is what they protect more than anything else.

The Emotional Life of the Non-Thinker

Non-thinkers live in emotional weather. Their moods shift with headlines, gossip, and circumstance. They react before they reflect, moved by whatever emotion is strongest at the moment. They are quick to anger, quick to fear, and quick to forget.

Because they do not examine their feelings, they are ruled by them. Desire drives their goals, fear sets their limits, and habit directs their days. They rarely ask why they feel as they do, or whether their feelings are justified. Emotion replaces reason, and impulse replaces choice.

This makes them easy to influence. Those who know how to stir emotion can lead non-thinkers anywhere , into conflict, into debt, into blind loyalty. History's tyrants, con men, and demagogues have always understood this. When people stop thinking, they become tools for others' ambitions.

The Daily Habits of Unthinking Lives

The lives of non-thinkers follow patterns of unconscious repetition. They wake, work, eat, and sleep in cycles that rarely change. Their routines fill time but do not build meaning. They rush from task to task, proud of being busy, yet unsure what all the motion is for.

Their days are governed by external forces , clocks, deadlines, and entertainment schedules. When one distraction ends, another begins. They fill silence with sound, conversation with chatter, and leisure with consumption. What they call relaxation is often escape from reflection.

Because they rarely think, they rarely learn. Experience teaches only those who reflect on it. The non-thinker suffers the same mistakes repeatedly, blaming circumstances rather than choices. They seek new jobs, partners, or places, but carry the same unexamined habits wherever they go.

The Social Behavior of Non-Thinkers

In groups, non-thinkers find safety. The presence of others shields them from doubt. The group thinks for them, deciding what is right and wrong. This collective comfort is powerful. It creates belonging, but it also breeds conformity.

Non-thinkers fear standing apart. They equate agreement with loyalty and silence with peace. When confronted with new ideas, they retreat behind familiar slogans. Group approval replaces self-respect.

They also crave validation. Compliments sustain them more than truth. They avoid those who challenge them, preferring the company of those who flatter or agree. This hunger for approval shapes every decision. They dress, speak, and even believe according to what earns applause.

The Economics of Non-Thinking

Modern economies depend on non-thinkers. They are the perfect consumers , impulsive, emotional, and easily persuaded. Advertising plays on their desires, promising happiness through purchase. They buy to feel better, not because they need.

Non-thinkers live beyond their means, chasing comfort today at the cost of freedom tomorrow. Debt becomes normal. They work harder to maintain the illusion of success, never realizing that the system is designed to keep them occupied but not independent.

Those who profit from distraction understand this cycle well. They sell entertainment that dulls reflection, news that provokes emotion, and products that soothe anxiety. The less people think, the more predictable their spending becomes.

The Non-Thinker and Responsibility

Responsibility demands reflection. To act responsibly, one must see consequences beyond the moment. Non-thinkers do not. They respond to the immediate , the impulse, the mood, the pressure. When problems arise, they blame others. When success happens, they call it luck.

Their relationships suffer for this reason. They make promises without thought and break them without guilt. They are surprised by outcomes that anyone thinking ahead could have foreseen. Without responsibility, trust erodes, and without trust, all relationships , personal, professional, civic , decay.

The Non-Thinker and Power

Non-thinkers rarely lead for long. When they do, they rule by fear or imitation, not understanding. Their decisions are reactive. They confuse control with competence and authority with wisdom. Because they do not question themselves, they cannot correct themselves.

In politics, they rise by repeating what the crowd wants to hear. They substitute charisma for clarity. They appeal to feeling instead of reason. And because many followers think the same way, they succeed , at least for a while. History shows the cost.

In organizations, non-thinking leaders resist innovation. They punish new ideas because new ideas expose their lack of depth. They value loyalty over truth, obedience over creativity. Under their rule, progress stalls until failure forces change.

The Private Life of the Non-Thinker

When the noise fades, the non-thinker feels emptiness. Entertainment can mask it for a time, but not erase it. Beneath the surface busyness lies a quiet ache , the sense that something essential is missing. That missing element is meaning.

Because they rarely examine themselves, non-thinkers live disconnected from their own purpose. They measure life by possessions or approval rather than by understanding. They seek comfort, but comfort without purpose becomes boredom.

Some sense the emptiness and try to fill it with more of the same , more distraction, more activity, more talk. Others simply resign. They stop expecting more from life because thinking would require admitting how much has been wasted.

The Consequences of a Thoughtless Society

When non-thinking becomes the norm, societies weaken. Laws multiply because conscience fades. Citizens trade freedom for convenience. Leaders exploit division because reflection has disappeared.

A society of non-thinkers cannot solve complex problems because it cannot agree on facts. It argues endlessly while reality deteriorates. It becomes easier to inflame emotion than to inform reason. The result is chaos disguised as freedom.

Education, once the training of thought, becomes credentialing without comprehension. Entertainment replaces art. News becomes performance. In such a culture, thinking feels like rebellion. Those who question are mocked as elitist or strange.

Recovering Thought in a Thoughtless Age

The cure for non-thinking begins with humility. To think, one must first admit ignorance. Most people refuse. They would rather appear certain than become wise. Yet wisdom starts with saying, "I do not know."

From humility comes curiosity. Curiosity awakens the mind. It asks, "Why?" and "How?" It reads, listens, and observes. It doubts what everyone else accepts. This is not cynicism; it is freedom.

The thinker's life begins where imitation ends. Each small act of reflection , questioning a belief, analyzing a choice, noticing a contradiction , chips away at the prison of habit. Thought reclaims territory one decision at a time.

The Thinker Among Non-Thinkers

A person who thinks in a world of non-thinkers often feels alone. They are misunderstood, sometimes resented. People may call them critical, strange, or arrogant. But thinking is not arrogance; it is responsibility. Someone must notice what others ignore.

The thinker's challenge is patience. You cannot force others to think. You can only model it. You can ask questions gently, offer clarity quietly, and live the results visibly. Over time, example speaks louder than argument.

Thinking is contagious in the presence of integrity. When others see peace, confidence, and consistency in a thinker's life, they begin to wonder why. Curiosity opens doors that argument never will.

The Cost and Reward of Thinking

The non-thinker's life seems easier. They glide along the surface while the thinker wrestles below it. Yet the cost of not thinking is greater than the cost of thought. The non-thinker pays with wasted years, shallow relationships, and dependence on others' opinions.

The reward of thought is freedom. A thinker may struggle, but their struggles lead somewhere. They make choices consciously, live deliberately, and sleep without the unease of self-deception. They may not be wealthier or more popular, but they are awake.

Non-thinkers live reactive lives, guided by emotion and imitation. They mistake comfort for peace, habit for wisdom, and motion for progress. Their world is shallow because their attention never dives below the surface.

Thinking transforms that world. It replaces confusion with clarity, dependence with freedom, and noise with understanding. The difference between the two lives is not circumstance but awareness.

The non-thinker lives as if life happens to them. The thinker lives as if life happens through them. Only one of those paths leads to fulfillment.

Chapter 11: Elevate Your Thinking and Life

To elevate your thinking is to rise above the noise that fills most minds, to move from reacting to directing, from wandering thought to deliberate creation. It means choosing the kind of mind you wish to live with every day, one that serves you rather than sabotages you.

Most people do not think at this level. They drift. Their thoughts are shaped by habit, by news cycles, by social influence, by the loudest or latest voice in their ear. The elevated thinker begins with awareness, noticing how thoughts form, how they repeat, and how they steer emotion and action. From that moment of noticing, transformation begins.

The first step upward is not intelligence or education but intention. You cannot control every thought that enters your mind, but you can control which ones you entertain. Like a host at the door, you decide who stays and who leaves.

The Choice to Rise

Thinking higher requires a decision, a quiet vow that you will no longer be content with shallow thinking or borrowed ideas. This decision must be renewed daily because the pull of ordinary thought is strong. Every distraction invites you back to the level of reaction, where emotion rules and reason sleeps.

To sustain elevation, cultivate rituals that remind you of your intention. Begin each morning with a few minutes of stillness or end each evening by reviewing your day. Ask yourself, Did I think clearly? Did I let emotion rule me? Did I act from understanding or impulse?

Each reflection becomes a rung on the ladder upward. Over time, those rungs form a habit of higher awareness, a mental altitude where perspective widens and clarity deepens.

Seeing Above the Crowd

Elevated thinkers learn to see the same world others see but from a higher vantage point. When a situation arises, they ask questions that lift their view.

Instead of "Who's to blame?" they ask, "What can be learned?"
Instead of "Why me?" they ask, "Why not me, and what now?"
Instead of "How can I win?" they ask, "How can this improve everyone involved?"

From that perspective, anger softens, fear loosens, and new options appear. Problems shrink to their true size, and opportunities become visible.

A manager who loses a major client can dwell in frustration or step above it, studying what the loss reveals about service, timing, or trust. The elevated choice is analysis, not anxiety.

Training the Mind

No one climbs by accident. Elevation comes through training, practice, and correction. Begin by catching yourself in small lapses of clarity. When you complain, pause and restate the thought in constructive form. When you assume, stop and verify. When you judge, ask for context.

Each correction refines your mental posture, the way good form refines an athlete's movement. At first it feels unnatural, then it becomes instinct.

To strengthen this training, keep a short record of your clearest and cloudiest moments. Note what conditions helped you think well, time of day, setting, mood, even diet. Patterns will emerge. You'll learn when your mind is sharp and when it needs rest.

Like muscles, thoughts grow through repetition and rest in balance. The more often you practice clarity, the faster it becomes your default state.

The Power of Elevated Association

Your company determines your altitude. Surround yourself with people who challenge your assumptions rather than reinforce them. The best minds question kindly but persistently. They make you justify, refine, and sometimes abandon your weaker ideas.

Conversations at this level are not debates to win but explorations to share. You may leave uncertain but enriched. That uncertainty is progress, it means your mind has stretched.

When elevated minds gather, creativity multiplies. Think of the cafés of Paris where writers exchanged drafts, or the quiet meetings of inventors trading prototypes. Each borrowed clarity and returned it improved.

Seek such company. Read authors whose thinking humbles you. Listen to those who've lived widely. Exposure to better thought expands your own vocabulary of ideas.

Balancing Humility and Confidence

Higher thinking demands both humility and confidence, humility to admit what you do not know, and confidence to act on what you do.

Humility protects you from arrogance, the illusion that your view is complete. Confidence protects you from paralysis, the fear that no view is safe. The balance between them creates mental poise, allowing reason and intuition to cooperate instead of compete.

A surgeon must be confident enough to operate, humble enough to keep learning. A teacher must be sure enough to lead, modest enough to revise their lesson when evidence changes. The same duality strengthens every thinker.

From Reaction to Creation

The ordinary mind reacts; the elevated mind creates. Reaction belongs to habit, creation to awareness.

When insulted, most people respond with equal heat. The elevated thinker pauses, analyzes, and chooses whether to respond, reframe, or remain silent. That pause is the birthplace of mastery. It changes not only the moment but the future, because it builds a pattern of control.

Over time, this habit turns thought into architecture. Instead of living inside mental noise, you design your inner environment. Anger becomes analysis, envy becomes inspiration, fear becomes preparation. Every emotion becomes raw material for growth.

The Language of Higher Thought

Words both express and shape thought. To think better, refine your language. Replace vague words with precise ones, instead of "bad," say "ineffective"; instead of "good," say "useful," "honest," or "kind." Precision disciplines the mind to see differences where laziness once saw sameness.

Avoid exaggeration and assumption. They inflate emotion and shrink understanding. Elevated thinkers speak in measured tones because they have nothing to prove and much to convey.

Practice rewriting impulsive phrases in calmer form. The difference between "This always fails" and "This often fails when rushed" is the difference between despair and insight.

Language builds thought the way bricks build walls. Lay them with care.

The Habit of Reflection

Reflection converts experience into wisdom. Without it, events pass through life like rain through sand, momentary and wasted.

At day's end, take ten minutes to review what went well, what didn't, and why. Ask not only what happened but what pattern it reveals. Patterns are the footprints of thought.

If you notice the same frustration repeating, look beneath it. Perhaps it hides an unchallenged assumption or a fear of change. Seeing the pattern weakens its grip.

Keep a small notebook for these reflections. Over months, it becomes a mirror showing the evolution of your mind. Nothing reveals growth like reading your former thoughts and realizing how much they have matured.

Practical Exercises for Elevated Thinking

1. Pause before opinion. When hearing news or gossip, wait ten seconds before reacting. Use that time to ask, What do I truly know?
2. Rephrase negativity. Convert complaints into questions, "Why is this so hard?" becomes "What could make this easier?"
3. Visualize thought as weather. Notice clouds of emotion passing through the sky of your mind. Don't chase them; observe them drift.
4. Mentally declutter. Once a week, list recurring thoughts. Cross out the useless ones. Focus only on thoughts tied to purpose.
5. Elevate through gratitude. Each morning, note three things that work well. Gratitude shifts attention from scarcity to abundance, lifting thought from complaint to creation.

Practiced daily, these small exercises compound like interest, building mental wealth that outlasts circumstance.

Living the Results

Elevated thinking produces visible changes. People will notice calm replacing hurry, clarity replacing chatter, composure replacing conflict. You will make fewer but better decisions, because your thoughts will be aligned with principle rather than pressure.

Material success may follow, but it is secondary. The deeper reward is internal order, the sense that your thoughts, emotions, and actions now pull in the same direction. That alignment generates peace no distraction can steal.

At this level, thinking becomes a form of service. Your clarity benefits others, your restraint diffuses tension, your insight helps guide those still finding their way. Elevation is contagious.

The Highest View

Ultimately, elevated thinking is not about superiority but perspective. It is seeing life from a height that includes compassion. You begin to notice how everyone struggles with the same raw materials of fear, hope, and uncertainty. Judgment softens into understanding.

From this vantage point, you realize that wisdom and kindness are twins. To think clearly is to care deeply, because clarity reveals connection. Every thought that uplifts the mind uplifts the world it touches.

In time, elevated thinking becomes a way of being rather than a skill. You stop trying to rise; you live aloft.

Chapter 12: Thinking in the Age of Artificial Intelligence

Artificial Intelligence has become the newest mirror of the human mind. It was born from our own patterns of reasoning and imitation, yet now it begins to influence the way we reason and imagine in return. In this sense, thinking and AI are no longer separate; they form a loop, each shaping the other. To understand thinking today, one must recognize how technology participates in it.

The Extension of Mind

For centuries, tools have extended human ability. The wheel extended motion, the lever extended strength, writing extended memory, and the transistor extended information processing. Artificial Intelligence extends thought itself. When we ask a system to summarize, predict, or create, we are outsourcing a fragment of our own reasoning. The difference is that this extension does not merely store what we know; it learns patterns and offers possibilities we may not have considered.

Used wisely, AI becomes a mental partner. It helps writers generate ideas, scientists test theories, and doctors analyze data too vast for one mind. But when the partnership is unbalanced, dependence replaces understanding. **The danger is not that AI will think for us, but that we will stop thinking as deeply ourselves.**

The Erosion of Attention

Thinking requires patience. It unfolds through focus, silence, and struggle. AI tools shorten that path. With predictive answers, instant suggestions, and endless access to surface knowledge, the modern mind learns to skim rather than dwell. The reward of effort , the satisfaction of finding meaning through search and reflection , begins to fade.

Consider how we now approach questions. In the past, we pondered, compared, and reasoned through competing ideas. Today, a single query produces an immediate response. Convenient, yes, but convenience is not the same as comprehension. **A thought gained without effort often fades as quickly as it arrives.**

To think well in the age of AI, we must protect our attention. We must preserve the ability to question beyond the first answer, to read beyond the summary, to feel the weight of uncertainty before reaching for resolution.

The Mirror of Bias

AI systems are built from human data, which means they inherit human flaws. They reflect the biases, assumptions, and shortcuts present in the societies that created them. When we rely on these systems to inform or guide thought, **we risk amplifying our own distortions under the illusion of objectivity.**

A search engine that predicts what we want to see, or a social feed that repeats what we already believe, narrows the mind's field of vision. True thinking widens it. An intelligent person uses AI as a tool for discovery, not validation. The difference lies in whether we ask it to confirm or to challenge.

The Temptation of Ease

Every invention changes the habits of the people who use it. The printing press spread knowledge but also made memorization less necessary. Calculators improved accuracy but weakened mental arithmetic. AI now automates language, logic, and creativity, the very functions that once defined thinking itself.

The danger of ease is that it feels harmless. When a program writes an essay, finishes a sentence, or paints an image, the product may seem impressive. Yet if we never engage in the act of creation ourselves, our mental muscles weaken. Thought, like the body, grows through exertion.

The wise user of AI treats it like a gym for the mind, not a substitute for it. **The goal is not to let the machine think, but to think better because of it.**

The Challenge of Originality

AI thrives on patterns. It learns from what has been said, drawn, or done before. It can recombine, refine, and extend those patterns, but it does not originate in the human sense of struggle, emotion, or lived experience. Its creativity is statistical, not spiritual.

For human thinkers, originality begins where pattern ends. It is the moment of surprise, of reaching beyond what data predicts. When we depend too heavily on generated answers, we risk losing that instinct for the unknown, the curiosity that drives invention and art.

The thinker who uses AI well remembers that **the most valuable ideas still come from the friction between doubt and insight. Machines can mimic, but they cannot marvel.**

The Human Responsibility

Every tool inherits the morality of its user. AI magnifies this truth. A single careless command can shape information, emotion, or influence across millions of people. The responsibility of thought, therefore, becomes heavier, not lighter.

We must train ourselves to question not only the output but the process. Who trained this system? What data shaped it? What purpose guides its design? These are not technical questions; they are moral ones. To think in the age of AI is to think about consequence, not only what we can do, but what we should do.

Intention and AI

AI cannot form its own intention. It can select from a list of goals provided to it, or someone can feed it a purpose, and, in such cases, it can "run with it" efficiently. But it cannot *decide* to have a goal. Intention arises from consciousness , from awareness of self, meaning, and consequence. AI has none of these. It does not desire, question, or choose in the human sense; it only executes instructions within parameters we define. This distinction matters because it reminds us that the danger of AI does not come from the machine itself, but from the human intentions behind it. A program cannot plot or conspire without direction; it only amplifies the motives of its creators and users. The threat, therefore, is not that AI will suddenly decide to take over the world, but that people will use it to pursue their own ambitions without restraint or wisdom.

Thinking as the Final Frontier

There is irony in our time. As we build machines to think faster, we must learn to think slower. As AI grows in power, human reflection becomes more valuable, not less. The future will not belong to those who copy what machines do best, but to those who do what machines cannot, imagine, empathize, and understand meaning beyond measurement.

The greatest thinkers of the coming age will not be those who reject AI or those who depend on it, but those who collaborate with it intelligently, using it as a mirror to refine their own reasoning. Artificial Intelligence can analyze, compare, and imitate, but only a human mind can assign purpose and value.

The art of thinking, therefore, remains our most important task. AI can extend it, amplify it, and even test it, but it cannot replace it. Machines may process information, but only humans can transform it into wisdom, and imagine ideas that reach beyond the limits of past knowledge and algorithmic extrapolation.

Chapter 13: Conclusion

Thinking well is not something that happens once and remains forever. It is a living practice that requires care, honesty, and renewal. The mind that guided you yesterday must be reviewed today, because both you and the world keep changing. Elevating your thinking, therefore, is not a single ascent but a continuous climb.

At the start of this journey, you learned that thinking defines who you are. Every choice, belief, and emotion grows out of what you allow to live in your mind. By learning to guide your thoughts, you learn to guide your life. That truth is simple but powerful enough to change everything.

You have seen how thinking can be trained like a skill. It improves with repetition, awareness, and correction. When you reflect, question, and clarify, you strengthen the muscles of the mind. When you allow laziness, distraction, or fear to take over, those muscles weaken. Every moment is an opportunity to start again.

Thought as Foundation

Behind every achievement lies an idea, and behind every idea, a thought that refused to remain ordinary. People build houses, companies, and movements, but before the first brick or step, someone had to imagine a better way. Thought is always the foundation.

To think better is to live better, not because thinking alone solves problems, but because it gives you control over the only instrument that never leaves you, your own mind. The disciplined thinker can face change without panic, temptation without surrender, and failure without despair. No one can guarantee comfort or safety, but anyone can learn steadiness.

The elevated thinker accepts that thought is responsibility. Ideas influence others; words shape futures. To think clearly and speak truthfully is an act of integrity. You become a quiet force for reason in a noisy world.

A Mind in Balance

Balanced thinking does not chase perfection. It recognizes that intellect and emotion must work together. You need logic to stay grounded and empathy to stay human. The goal is not to silence feeling but to make it a partner of reason.

A well-ordered mind has room for both firmness and compassion. It can hold opposing ideas long enough to find truth between them. It knows when to speak and when silence carries greater strength. That calm balance is what others will come to trust in you.

The Journey Beyond This Book

The chapters of this book are not lessons to be memorized but mirrors to be revisited. Each time you return to them, you will see something new, because you will have changed. Your experiences, challenges, and triumphs will reshape how the same words sound.

Thinking well is like tuning an instrument. Even a well-tuned mind drifts slightly with time and use. Reflection is how you tighten the strings again, restoring clarity and harmony. When you feel confusion or fatigue creeping in, go back to the basics, pause, observe, question, clarify, and refocus.

You do not need to think about everything deeply, only about what matters most. Use your energy wisely. Save your mental power for things that build, heal, and improve. The rest can pass through without attention. Simplicity, not complexity, is the mark of mature thought.

A Life of Deliberate Awareness

Living with deliberate awareness means carrying your thinking into every ordinary act. You eat, walk, speak, and listen with attention. You choose words that help, decisions that align, and habits that serve. You become more intentional and less reactive.

That awareness changes relationships. You begin to notice what others need instead of what they do wrong. You hear what is meant, not just what is said. You give more grace to mistakes, your own and others', because you see that thinking is a process for everyone, not a finished product.

As you practice, you will find that peace grows not from control but from clarity. You may still face conflict, but you will face it with steadiness. You will still feel emotion, but it will no longer drown reason. You will still meet failure, but you will learn from it faster and rise sooner.

The End as a Beginning

Every ending invites reflection, and this one is no different. You have read about thought as energy, habit, choice, and skill. You have learned that thinking better begins with self-awareness and ends with service, using your clarity to better the lives around you.

But this conclusion is not an end. It is an opening, an invitation to apply what you know. Begin by noticing how you think today, then decide how you wish to think tomorrow. Small improvements compound into transformation.

Do not wait for perfect conditions or total confidence. Start where you are, with the next thought you have. Choose to elevate it, to question it, refine it, or replace it with one that brings more truth and peace. Every improved thought improves your life.

Final Thoughts

The world changes faster than any single mind can track, but the power to think clearly remains timeless. It is the one resource that never loses value, the one tool that cannot be taken from you unless you neglect it.

Think deliberately. Think kindly. Think with purpose. Let your thoughts build the kind of life that reflects who you are at your best.

You began this book as a thinker among many. If you apply what you have learned, you will end it as a thinker among the few, someone who understands that the greatest form of intelligence is not to know everything, but to think honestly about what is known.

And that is how every life, and every world, begins to change.

Chapter 14: Exercises

These exercises are designed to strengthen your ability to think clearly, calmly, and independently. They require no special materials or environment, only honesty and persistence. Use them as a weekly or monthly discipline. Repetition will turn them into habits, and habits will reshape your thinking.

1. The Observation Exercise

Spend five minutes observing something simple: a tree, a cup of coffee, a person walking by. Avoid labeling or judging; simply notice. Describe what you see in complete sentences, either aloud or in writing.
Then ask yourself, "What did I assume?" and "What did I overlook?"
This practice teaches you the first rule of thought, seeing without distortion. You will discover how quickly the mind adds opinion to fact and how powerful it is to remove it.

2. The Reflection Log

At the end of each day, write three short entries:

1. What I thought well today.
2. What I thought poorly or carelessly about.
3. What I will think differently tomorrow.
   Keep it brief and consistent. This single habit will sharpen awareness more effectively than any lecture on thinking. Reflection is the mirror of progress.

3. The Question Chain

Take a belief or opinion you hold strongly and write it at the top of a page. Then ask "Why?" below it and write your answer. Under that answer, ask "Why?" again. Continue until you reach five layers deep or until no further answer appears.
This reveals the roots of your thinking, where beliefs come from and whether they rest on evidence, habit, or emotion. The chain teaches humility and strengthens logic.

4. The Reversal Test

When faced with a problem, reverse it. Instead of asking, "How can I succeed?" ask, "What would guarantee failure?" List those answers. Then do the opposite.
This reversal often exposes hidden assumptions and lazy patterns. It transforms vague hopes into specific actions. Many creative breakthroughs begin this way.

5. The Stillness Minute

Sit quietly for one minute, focusing on your breathing. When a thought enters, notice it, label it "thought," and let it go. Do not fight it or follow it. Return attention to breathing. This simple practice builds metacognition, the ability to see thoughts instead of being trapped in them. One minute of clarity can reset an entire day.

6. The Word Audit

Choose a paragraph you have written or a conversation you remember well. Recreate it on paper and highlight words that are vague or emotional, such as "always," "never," "terrible," or "amazing." Replace them with more accurate terms.
By refining your words, you refine your mind. Precision of language forces precision of thought.

7. The Perspective Shift

Think of a disagreement you've had. Write your own view in one paragraph. Then, in the next paragraph, argue the opposite side as sincerely and persuasively as possible.
This exercise trains empathy and expands understanding. You may not change your conclusion, but you will understand the reasoning of others more deeply. A good thinker sees from both sides before judging either.

8. The Focus Drill

Choose one ordinary task, such as washing dishes, folding laundry, or walking, and do it with full attention. Notice each movement, sound, and sensation. When your mind drifts, bring it back without frustration.
This trains concentration. A mind that can stay on one task can stay on any task. Over time, your focus will lengthen, and clarity will come more easily.

9. The Gratitude Reframe

List three problems that frustrate you. Under each, write one hidden benefit or lesson it brings. For example, "My job is stressful" may reveal "It's teaching me patience and boundaries."
Reframing trains your mind to look beyond complaint toward meaning. It builds resilience, the foundation of emotional intelligence.

10. The Reading Reflection

After finishing a book, article, or video, write a one-sentence summary of what it truly meant, not just what it said.

Then write one way you can apply it.
This exercise prevents passive consumption. It turns information into insight, and insight into action.

11. The Weekly Reset

Once a week, step away from routine. Take an hour without screens, music, or conversation. Walk, sit outdoors, or simply rest. Let your mind wander freely, but keep a notepad nearby. Record any thought that repeats or feels important. These unguarded insights often reveal what your deeper mind has been trying to tell you. Many of life's best decisions appear during these quiet resets.

12. The Mentorship Map

List five people, living or dead, whose thinking you respect. Beside each name, write what you admire, such as clarity, courage, creativity, or compassion. Then ask, "Which of these traits do I practice least, and how can I strengthen it?" Learning from the great minds of others is not imitation; it is acceleration. Their examples can pull you upward faster than solitary effort.

13. The Decision Review

After each major decision, career, family, financial, or personal, review the process, not just the outcome. Ask, "Did I gather enough facts? Did I let emotion interfere? Did I consult the right people? Did I reflect before acting?"
Document what you learn. Over time, your decision-making will become more consistent and objective, guided by patterns you can trust.

14. The Silence Test

Spend one day each month speaking as little as possible. Observe how others react, how your own mind fills the space, and what you learn from listening instead of talking.
Silence reveals how much energy we waste explaining, defending, or reacting. It teaches restraint and deepens perception.

15. The Life Audit

At the end of each season, review four areas of life: mental, emotional, physical, and relational. For each, write one strength, one weakness, and one improvement.
This quarterly check keeps your life aligned with your values. You will notice that improvement in thinking always leads to improvement in living.

Thinking better begins with observation and ends with transformation. Each of these exercises is a doorway to greater self-awareness, focus, and peace. Do them not as chores but as invitations to clarity. The mind you shape through practice will become the life you live through choice.

In time, these exercises will no longer feel like exercises. They will become part of how you think, how you see, and how you are. And that is the true reward of learning to think deliberately, the discovery that your best thoughts are already within you, waiting to be chosen.

Appendix I: Questions to Change Your Life

Good questions are tools that cut through confusion. They expose assumptions, open perspective, and lead to self-awareness. Each question in this section is designed to help you think more deeply, act more wisely, and live more deliberately.

Set aside quiet time to consider a few at a time. Write your answers if possible. The point is not speed but honesty.

Questions About Awareness

1. What are my three most common thoughts each day, and do they serve or drain me?
2. When I am quiet, what do I usually think about first?
3. What emotion most often shapes my decisions?
4. How often do I pause before reacting?
5. What habits or distractions most often steal my focus?
6. What would my life look like if I directed my thoughts with more care?

Questions About Purpose

1. What truly matters to me when no one is watching?
2. If I stopped trying to impress others, what would I pursue?
3. Which activities make me lose track of time in a good way?
4. What values guide my best choices, and do I live by them consistently?
5. What would I do differently if I believed I could not fail?
6. How do I define success in one clear sentence?

Questions About Belief

1. Which of my opinions have I never questioned?
2. What evidence supports what I believe, and what evidence challenges it?
3. Who or what has shaped my beliefs the most?
4. When was the last time I changed my mind because of new information?
5. How do I respond when someone disagrees with me, and what does that reveal?

Questions About Relationships

1. Do I listen to understand or to reply?
2. What qualities in others inspire me, and which challenge me?
3. Who in my life makes me think more clearly and kindly?
4. Where do I still carry resentment, and why have I kept it?
5. What does respect look like in my words and actions?
6. How can I express appreciation more often and more sincerely?

Questions About Growth

1. What lesson keeps repeating in my life, and what am I avoiding learning?
2. When do I feel most alive and alert?
3. How do I handle criticism, and what does that say about my security?
4. What skill or subject excites me enough to study on my own?
5. If I could ask my future self for advice, what question would I ask?
6. What small step today would make tomorrow easier or better?

Questions About Leadership and Influence

1. How do I use my influence, even in small ways?
2. Do people feel stronger or smaller after talking with me?
3. What example do I set in times of stress or disagreement?
4. How can I lead through clarity and calm instead of control?
5. What legacy do I want to leave in the lives I touch?

Questions About Meaning and Direction

1. What kind of world do I want to help create?
2. What do I want my daily routine to say about my priorities?
3. How do I want to be remembered by those closest to me?
4. Which moments in my life have felt most aligned with who I truly am?
5. What is one area where I am ready to stop surviving and start improving?
6. What does living with purpose mean to me right now, in this season of life?

These questions are not riddles to solve but doors to open. Each answer you uncover, even the uncertain ones, brings you closer to self-understanding. Return to them often. Your answers will evolve as you do.

The mind grows stronger not only by collecting facts but by asking better questions. Keep asking, keep noticing, and let every question become an invitation to think more clearly and live more fully.

Appendix II: Books to Read

Dimnet recommended a collection of books and authors that every serious thinker should be familiar with. A few additional titles have been included to broaden the scope for modern readers who value both classical and practical insight.

How to Live on Twenty-Four Hours a Day, Arnold Bennett
The Vicar of Wakefield, Oliver Goldsmith
The Iliad and *The Odyssey*, Homer
Works of Plato
Paradise Lost, John Milton
Works of Jean Racine
The Aeneid, Virgil
Parallel Lives, Plutarch
Demosthenes, Georges Clemenceau
The Divine Comedy, Dante Alighieri
Robinson Crusoe, Daniel Defoe
Vanity Fair, William Makepeace Thackeray
Wuthering Heights, Emily Brontë
The Arabian Nights, Anonymous
Evelina, Frances Burney
Le Misanthrope, Molière
The Hero with a Thousand Faces, Joseph Campbell
The plays of William Shakespeare
The *Sherlock Holmes* mysteries, Sir Arthur Conan Doyle
All works, including poems, by Edgar Allan Poe
Seven Pillars of Wisdom, T. E. Lawrence
All poems and stories by Rudyard Kipling

REFERENCES

Almendrala, Anna. "You Can Be Completely Mentally Alert While in a Coma." *Healthy Living*, 15 Jan. 2015, http://www.huffingtonpost.com/2015/01/15/locked-insyndrome_n_6474274.html. Accessed 30 June 2017.

Bierce, Ambrose. *The Devil's Dictionary.* Oxford University Press, 1999.

"Lucille Ball Quotes." *BrainyQuote*, https://www.brainyquote.com/quotes/quotes/l/lucillebal122757.html. Accessed 1 Aug. 2017.

"Are Buddhists Less Judgmental." *Quora*, https://www.quora.com/Are-Buddhists-less-judgemental. Accessed 1 Aug. 2017.

Camp, Jim. "The Science of Asking Great Questions." *American Management Association*, 27 June 2017, http://www.amanet.org/training/articles/The-Science-of-Asking-Great-Questions.aspx. Accessed 27 June 2017.

Church, Ellen Booth. "Scientific Thinking Step by Step." *Scholastic Blog*, 2017, https://www.scholastic.com/teachers/articles/teaching-content/scientific-thinking-step-step/. Accessed 27 June 2017.

Cirillo, Francesco. "The Pomodoro Technique." *Cirillo Company*, 2013, https://cirillocompany.de/pages/pomodorotechnique. Accessed 27 June 2017.

"Creative Thinking." *Business Dictionary*, http://www.businessdictionary.com/definition/creative-thinking.html. Accessed 27 June 2017.

Csikszentmihályi, Mihaly. *Flow: The Psychology of Optimal Experience.* Harper & Row, 1990. ISBN 978-0-06-016253-5. Wikipedia, https://en.wikipedia.org/wiki/Flow_(psychology). Accessed 27 June 2017.

"Decision Making." *University of Kent Careers and Employability Service,* https://www.kent.ac.uk/careers/sk/decisionmaking.htm. Accessed 27 June 2017.

Dimnet, Ernest. *The Art of Thinking.* Simon and Schuster, 1928. Print.

Drew. "Top 10 Geniuses of All Time." *Waking Times,* 1 Aug. 2012, http://www.wakingtimes.com/2012/08/01/top-50-geniuses-of-all-time/. Accessed 1 Aug. 2017.

"Albert Einstein Quotes." *BrainyQuote,* https://www.brainyquote.com/quotes/quotes/a/alberteins106912.html. Accessed 1 Aug. 2017.

"ADHD Symptoms: Hyperfocus." *Healthline,* http://www.healthline.com/health/adhd/adhd-symptoms-hyperfocus. Accessed 1 Aug. 2017.

Sullivan, Bob, and Thompson, Hugh. "Brain Interrupted." *The New York Times,* 3 May 2013, http://www.nytimes.com/2013/05/05/opinion/sunday/a-focus-on-distraction.html. Accessed 27 June 2017.

Tilus, Grant. "Critical Thinking Skills You Need to Master Now." *Rasmussen College Blog,* 12 Dec. 2013, http://www.rasmussen.edu/studentlife/blogs/main/critical-thinking-skills-you-need-to-master-now/. Accessed 27 June 2017.

"Vitamin D." *Reference*, https://www.reference.com/health/normal-vitamin-d-levelb5979e7ec283d98e?qo=cdpArticles. Accessed 27 June 2017.

Vrabie, Alina. "The Science Behind Concentration and Improved Focus." *Sandglaz Blog*, 6 Dec. 2013, http://blog.sandglaz.com/the-science-behind-concentration/. Accessed 27 June 2017.

Vrabie, Alina. "How to Improve Your Time Management Skills with the Urgent-Important Matrix." *Sandglaz Blog*, 3 June 2014, http://blog.sandglaz.com/the-urgent-important-matrix/. Accessed 27 June 2017.

ALSO BY CHARLES PATTON

• **For Honest Citizens Only**

A bold call for Americans to rise above politics and rebuild civic integrity.

• **In Defense of the Righteous**

A gripping story of moral courage when justice and survival collide.

• **Tigers of the Ice**

Adventure meets survival in an unforgiving world where instinct rules.

• **Mastering Strategy**

The essential guide to thinking, planning, and winning in any field.

• **Artificial Consciousness**

Explores the frontier of automating consciousness.

• **The Gardener's Secret and Other Stories**

Mysteries and dramas revealing the hidden motives behind ordinary lives.

• **Extreme Leadership**

What real leaders do when the stakes are high.

• **Who Do You Trust**

A deadly game of deceit between two spies and one truth.

• **Busted, What's Wrong With My Excuse**

An entertaining look at excuses people make, and how to excuse better.

• **Naked Reflections**

Raw, honest poetry of truth, ego, and the search for authenticity.

• **Charles Patton, Visionaire**

Insights from a lifetime of ideas, invention, and fearless creativity.

• **Storming the Castle Bridge**

A tale of rebellion, loyalty, and the unbreakable human will to be free.

Find every title at: charlespattonbooks.com